Ceramic Extruding:
Inspiration & Technique

Tom Latka and Jean Latka

Tom Latka, Women Dala, 2' x 2', 1999, made with fused glass, commercial tiles, and extruded accents, reduction cone 10.

Published by

krause publications

700 E. State St.
Iola, WI 54990-0001
Telephone 715-445-2214
www.krause.com

Please call or write for our free catalog. Our toll-free number to place an order or obtain a free catalog is 800-258-0929 or please use our regular business telephone 715-445-2214 for editorial comment and further information.

Library of Congress Catalog Number: 00-111290

ISBN: 0-87341-903-0

Printed in the United States of America

Unless indicated otherwise, all photos and illustrations are by Tom Latka.

This book is dedicated to Eleanor Rose Coon Scott Briggs for her unyielding belief and support. To artist Nick Latka, who left us far too soon. To Rose, Paris, and Westley for their finely crafted spirits. To the spirit of the people who have always done this work. It is from them we have learned this craft, a craft as old as clay and fire.

The entrance to Tom and Jean Latka's home and studio features an extruded brick driveway.

Table of Contents

The Hand, the Material, and the Technology

An amazing number of fascinating objects have been made from clay throughout history. This is no doubt due to human ingenuity, but also to the abundance and accessibility of clay as a natural material spread over the entire surface of the globe. Clay requires only the simple process of applying sufficient heat to render it permanent. Thus, when fired, clay has become containers for cooking and serving food, bricks for building houses, tiles for embellishing walls, and raw material for sculpture celebrating culture and the human spirit. In ceramic history, the relationship between the hand, the materials, and the technology has been a crucial one.

Ancient peoples made their pots by hand processes long before the development of the potter's wheel. Whenever possible, however, the incentive has been to speed up or simplify the process of making, inventing, and using tools specifically designed for that purpose. Looking at the continuum of such tools, one can see that a long list of increasingly specific tools has been developed to assist the potter in making objects of utility and beauty. First was the potter's hand, fashioning coils and slabs into round shapes long before the wheel became the accepted tool for hollowing out balls of clay. The hand was assisted by shaping and scoring tools of wood, bone, or stone, with paddles for beating and giving texture to the clay, with brushes for applying color, and carving instruments and objects to press into the clay for texture. Conceptually viewed, the rock and paddle of Peru became the Native American *puki* bowl. The *puki* became the cartwheel lying on its side to be spun by a twist of a stick. The cartwheel became the potter's wheel powered by foot or with electricity. The mold into which clay was pressed became the slab roller, the jigger, and the jolly. The slab roller became the toggle press, the fly press, and the ram press. The ram press became the extruder for making more complex noncircular clay shapes. And extruder shapes gave rise to computer-generated forms for a virtual clay reality.

This impetus for tools to become forms of mechanization inevitably led to angst and conflict among its practitioners. The handcraft revival movement of the 1880s - of which we are all legatees - was a rebellion among artists and critics against the spread of machine-made objects, and against the ugliness of Victorian taste. Led in England by William Morris, the movement urged people to join in a revival of handcrafts that could assist in surviving the detested machine and its materialistic world.

While potters have always been artists in an unselfconscious sense, there was a shift away from pots made for use to pots made for art. Morris' movement, attempting to restore the past, led crafts instead in the direction of the fine arts, a direction that perhaps Morris and others could not foresee. This resulted in changes in the social status of the potter and led to conflicts not wholly resolved today. It became difficult for the art school graduate to become an unsophisticated village potter. The apprentice became the student, the workshop the studio, the shop the gallery. Pots became ceramics, the potter became the artist. And everyone's prices went up.

The question arises: What is a tool? When is a tool a machine? At what point does mechanics interfere with the work of the hand and the spirit? There are no easy answers to these questions and surely each potter has opinions based on pragmatic decisions. While it is true that most people in the world enjoy the benefits of mass-produced china pottery without too much pain, some potters remain perplexed by these philosophical conundrums. Nevertheless, the individual potter continues with honesty and integrity to produce pots made as single works of art done with whatever tools are available. Generally, the extruder has been accepted today as a practical and beneficial tool in the studio.

In 1981 several professional potters met to conduct an evaluation of commercial extruders for *The Studio Potter Journal*. As they pulled down the handles on the 15 or 20 instruments under consideration and examined the quality of the extruded clay, they gave their assessments. Their evaluation was almost uniformly positive about the usefulness of extruders in the studio. What they said is worth repeating here.

The great challenge, they said, lies in designing products for this new tool. The hard part is in trying not to imitate thrown or slab forms but to develop forms specifically for the extruder. The extruder is not just a tool to use because of an idea, but should provoke the idea, and be the genesis of the idea. They urged potters to avoid mindless duplication of inane and thoughtless pots, which can happen with wheel work, too. Because of the inevitable similarity to throwing, they urged potters to think horizontally, assembling square, rectangles, or other geometric shapes which are away from the vertical. The extruder gives the potter freedom to explore, to be adventuresome, and to open up new areas of work. They felt that the use of the extruder, together with the slab roller, was a healthy development helping to destroy old myths. Great things could come from tools with no cultural traditions behind them. They said: Let the imagination run wild!

This advice, given 20 years ago, was useful to many potters weighing the option of the extruder as a tool for studio work. Much more needed to be said, however. Here is a reference text for both the beginner and the professional, written by practicing artists with great experience. I cannot help but wish I had the advantage of such a text when I first started working with the extruder. May this opportunity be the beginning of new work for you, and a challenge to your imagination, as you enter or further explore the world just around the corner.

Gerry Williams
Studio Potter Journal
Goffstown, New Hampshire

Introduction

We once asked Michael Cardew, at age 76, why he became a potter. He replied, "I couldn't do anything else." Meaning that he had no choice - that it was his destiny.

We feel that our lives have also been so blessed and directed.

The extruding pugmill is our machine of choice.

Though the words "extrude" and "extrusion" are not ones most people encounter in everyday conversation, we live in a world where we are surrounded by extruded objects. Our brick houses and their tile roofs are made from extruded clay. We shower on extruded tiles, send our smoke and fumes up extruded chimneys, and our waste down extruded sewers. From the round O's in our breakfast cereal to the pasta on our dinner plates, extruded objects occupy every conceivable nook and cranny of our lives.

But what is this extrusion process? Basically, an extruder is a machine that forces a material down a barrel and through a shape called a die. The material then takes the shape of that die. The extruder is versatile in its ability to produce forms, shapes, and slabs with ease and fluid motion. For us, the extruded form is only the starting point. From there we expand the forms with hand-building, throwing, and extreme manipulation, pushing the mechanical shapes into the organic world and ending with clean crisp lines that flow like a river.

The industrial production world makes the most of the extruding process by forcing a variety of materials such as steel, rubber, plastic, clay, and aluminum through specialty dies to create a variety of products. Wire, glue sticks, engine parts, hair barrettes, bolts, food, and train rails are just a few examples that demonstrate how the extrusion process has secured its place in our urban infrastructure.

Given its fluidity and ease for mass production it is not surprising that clay was one of the first materials to be extruded. In the early part of the 18th century, brick manufacturers quickly incorporated extruding into their methods. As the centuries churned past, clay extrusions became more refined, gracing the facades of skyscrapers that towered over our cities during the 1940s.

In the past 30 years the extruder's role has expanded from a machine intended for mass production to a tool considered by many clay artists to be a necessary piece of studio equipment.

Many production potteries employ the extruder to produce quantities of objects that are the same shape. With some of these objects, like handles, extrusion is only one step in the production process, while for other objects, like tiles, the extruded form is practically the end step in their

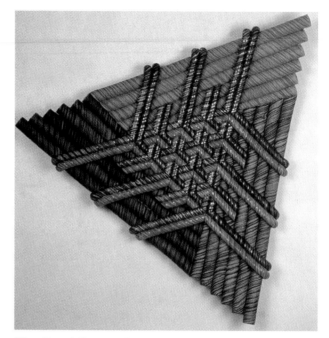

Elina Brandt-Hansen, Colored Triangle, 20" x 20", 1995. "The invention of so many layers of surface that take one down into the very fabric of the pieces, sits there waiting to be discovered." Photo by Les Blakebrough.

Tom Latka and Jean Latka, Teleconnect. Mural, 12' x 8', 1998, made with commercial tile reglazed, extruded, and carved, clay, glass, and stone, cone 01.

fabrication. The clay sculptor has also embraced the extruder, proclaiming that the tool provides a new artistic dimension to their work. Exploration into the creative potential of the extruder has never been as accessible as it is today.

We brought the pugmill into our studio initially to cut down on the amount of time we spent wedging clay. Cursed

Los Angeles Theater, building facade made from extruded clay forms. Photo from the archives of Gladding McBean.

Jack Sures, Sturdy Stone Building Mural, 2900 square feet, 1979, mural background made from extruded tiles, 9" x 12", the 32' diameter from carved brick, reduction cone 10. Photo by the artist.

with an inefficient bread dough mixer to blend our clay formula, we found ourselves devoting much of the morning wedging the clay in preparation for the day's throwing. Exhausted and looking for ways to expedite the routine procedures in the studio, we purchased a pugmill, placed it horizontally on a table and began pugging. The results were fabulous and our wrists were thankful.

One day while visiting with Cardew, he noticed the pugmill and commented that the English tradition is to mount the pugmill vertically on the wall. In this manner the pugged clay exits the machine freely, using gravity to assist the process, because the pugged clay doesn't encounter the friction of a table as is typical when it rests horizontally.

Recognizing the good sense in this suggestion, we mounted our pugmill vertically to a post in the studio. The pugging was faster and easier and the amount of studio floor space made available was wonderful. We had managed to combine ease and efficiency.

Shortly afterwards, we started making various dies and incorporated them into our pottery repertoire. Our pugmill had become an extruder. We extruded handles for mugs, massive coils for lips on giant pots, wide cylinders to cut open for slabs, hollow shapes for vases, and abstract shapes to construct sculptural forms. We had modified a standard machine to encompass and expand our clay production and creativity.

As our enthusiasm for this tool abounded so did our excitement when we discovered other clay artists experimenting and using the extruder in their work. It is our intention in this book to introduce you to some of the most skilled, creative, and talented artists working with the extruder today. The rich diversity of their work is dazzling and together they offer a wide range of form, color, and artistic vision, each one created from a machine that has been around since the early 1800s. These artists have invented new methods and equipment to express their ideas and we feel these inventions and objects will contribute to the ever-expanding history of ceramics.

Tom Latka   Jean Latka

Chapter 1
A Brief History of Extruders

Historically speaking, the extruder has evolved through a long and rich process, but to truly appreciate its historical significance and development, it is necessary to look briefly at the history of brick, because it was the search for a more expedient method of brick production that eventually led to the studio extruder.

Brick follows man's rise from adobe structures to skyscrapers and has played a leading role in all civilizations. Brick is the common thread that links the constructs of the world, from the ancient walls of Jericho to the modern building in your neighborhood.

When ancient man made shelters of dried mud and slabs of split rock, he used the available natural resources that did not entail any manufacturing process. In lands lacking forests or stone quarries the inhabitants were forced to seek other materials with which to erect permanent shelters. Modern Iran, the home of ancient Mesopotamia, is believed to be the birth place of clay products. Here, between the banks of the Tigris and Euphrates, men squatted and shaped the first bricks from river clay. Set out in the hot sun and dried hard, the bricks were used to construct huge temples, inns, houses, and palaces.

Brick-making is one of the oldest professions known to man. It is mentioned in the Bible book of Genesis, "Go, let us make brick and burn them. And they had brick for stone and slime they had for mortar." Another passage from Exodus 18 tells of a command from the Pharaoh, "Off to work, then! Straw shall not be provided for you but your tally of brick shall remain the same."

Brick has been traced back 10,000 years from the archeological digs beneath the city of Jericho. In the ruins of the biblical city of Abraham, inscriptions in the brick walls tell us much of daily life in those days. It was Nebuchadnezzar, the King of Kings, in the 6th century B.C. who built his glorious city of Babylon, with its towering 40-foot gateways, colossal arches, great temples, broad buttresses, and immense palaces - all from sun dried brick.

It is estimated that terracotta fired brick became the norm about 5,000 years ago and was immediately integrated into the building culture. Early bricks were 13" x 13" x 3" and weathered so well that they actually became harder as they aged. As civilizations such as the Greeks and Egyptians rose and fell, each reused the bricks from the previous settlement. Bricks unearthed in 1953 in Athens, 3,500 years after they were made, were declared fit for reuse.

The Romans, who ruled and pillaged the ancient world, left two important legacies: law and brick-making. Law provided the stability and structure necessary to the founding of industry and brick-making was one of the first industries.

Multicolored clays extruded together, creating a variegated colored commercial floor tile. Each tile is 4" x 9".

With their organizational genius, the Romans propelled the industrial brick-making process across the western world. Their bricks were hand-molded, beaten flat, trimmed, and glazed on both sides. They were used to build walls to protect military camps and settled lands from invading tribes. The Romans were renowned for their road systems, constructing over 51,000 miles of roads at the height of the Empire, many made of brick and still in use today.

In 407 A.D. the tables turned and Rome became a city under siege. In a desperate attempt to defend the city from invading Goths, Vandals, and Huns, legions of Romans were called home and they brought with them the brick-makers. For the next seven centuries, brick-making came to a halt throughout Europe and anything made of brick during that time was built of reclaimed Roman brick.

Ken Williams, School Administration Building Mural, 9' x 167', 1978, made from carved brick, oxidation cone 6. Photo by the artist.

While Western civilization was busy discovering the value of working with brick, the Chinese of legendary Cathay were creating their own brick inspirations. Few realize that the Great Wall of China, 1,500 miles long and averaging 20 feet high and 13 feet thick, is built of brick. The Forbidden City of Peking, last home of the Manchu emperors, is a maze of walls, all brick.

Around 1125 A.D., a reawakening Europe climbed out of the disastrous Middle Ages and rediscovered the art of making bricks. The Low Countries of Belgium and Holland, lacking timber and stone resources, are credited with rediscovering the valuable architectural material. Soon churches, castles, and guildhalls filled the cities and countrysides and brick manufacturing became a major industry. This momentum carried across Europe and into England where prisoners of victorious English knights were forced to make bricks for such illustrious residences as Tattershall Castle, Lincolnshire, and Giffords Hall, all of which still stand today.

As nations expanded their boundaries during the 14th, 15th, and 16th centuries, brick-making was carried along, moving westward to the American colonies and Canada. In 1612 the Mayflower carried bricks in the hull as ballast. These bricks were later used in the foundations of the first Plymouth Rock buildings. George Washington's Virginia birthplace, the original White House, and the law office where Abe Lincoln began his career are structures using early brick.

There are records of brick plants in New Amsterdam, which is now New York, as early as 1628, and in 1667 the Massachusetts Court passed legislation to regulate the size and manufacture of brick. The size was dictated by what would fit comfortably in a man's hand.

In 1684 William Penn instructed his agents to build prin-

Raymond Elozua, Water Tank, 17" x 9" x 9", 1999, Bailey Pneumatic extruder used to extrude strips as small as ⅛" and upwards to create scale size clay "lumber." The wet stumps were assembled with slip and the entire structure was fired intact to cone 04. Photo by James Dee.

What Speckstruyff's pugmill may have looked like.

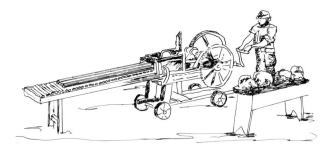
An early manual plunger-type extruder making hollow core bricks.

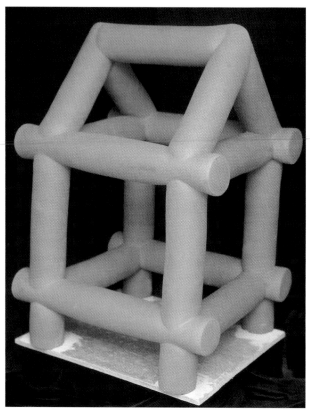
Robert Harrison, Extruded House, 60" x 48" x 40", 1981, extruded stoneware clay, oxidation cone 3. Photo by the artist.

Bailey power extruder.

"Extrusion is a very versatile process. The introduction of it on a wider scale adds an extra dimension to studio ceramics. A great many ideas can be more easily realized using this process, and this in turn can result in the more imaginative development of forms."

Oliver Bulley

cipally with brick and in 1692 the General Court of Boston passed an act requiring all new buildings more than 8 feet long and 7 feet high to be constructed of brick or stone.

It is important to recognize that all the brick made up to this time had been hand-molded. There were no machines to aid brick-makers in acquiring, processing, or shaping the clay. It was strictly a hand-labor business and it was a slow, arduous process. As the demand for brick increased, so did the desire to develop machinery that would produce quantities of brick more efficiently and expediently.

In 1643, a Dutchman, J.J. Speckstruyff, developed the first pugmill, a cone-shaped wooden tub with a revolving vertical shaft which had knives attached horizontally to it. It was powered by a horse harnessed to a pole that attached to the top of the shaft. The horse walked in a circle, the pole passing over the heads of the people in the middle who were

Sculpture by Alessio Tasca, stoneware, 4' x 4' x 18". Extrusion from large industrial extruder. Photo by A. Tasca.

William Shinn, Oval Fugue, 30" x 20" x 5", 2000, the cross-section of extruded clay used to unique advantage. Photo by the artist.

Oliver Bulley's Clay Bulley. Photo courtesy of O. Bulley.

Oliver Bulley, Three Bowls, 6" x 6" x 3", 1970, extruded from a die offset from the center, oxidation cone 6. Photo courtesy of the artist.

feeding aged clay into the machine. As the clay passed through the knives, it became more uniform and workable before being pushed through an opening at the side of the barrel, near the bottom. From here the clay was pressed into molds, dried, and fired. Speckstruyff's pugmill made it possible to produce 5,000 bricks a day and was considered state-of-the-art.[1]

It is believed that some version of Speckstruyff's pug-

Cumella's 1963 mural for the New York World's Fair. Photo by Agnes Vendrell de Cumella.

Shuji Ikeda, Basket, 14" x 14" x 9", 1999, extruded black and red stoneware clay using the small coil die. Photo by the artist.

Walter Keeler, Jug with Extruded Handle, 12" x 9" x 9", 1998, salt glaze, cone 10. Photo by the artist.

mill accompanied the colonists to the New World and was used to produce bricks for the early settlement of Williamsburg. The potteries in the Virginia area constructed similar mills to homogenize their clay before throwing the jugs and vessels typical of Early American pottery.

This rudimentary pugmill churned throughout the next century until the advent of the Industrial Revolution and the invention of steam power. Animal-driven mills were retired and a new machine age brought endless inventions that transformed the ancient art of brick-making.

In 1800, the first patent in the United States for brick machines was issued to George Hadfield. This early machine could produce 30,000 brick in 12 hours using only one horse. (By comparison, brick machines today produce 30,000 bricks an hour using 700 horsepower.)[2]

German Karl Schlickeysen combined the pugmill idea with Archimedes' invention of the auger 2,000 years earlier. Achimedes had undertaken to move water from a lower plain onto a higher one. He designed a giant helical screw carved from wood and attached this apparatus to the end to a horse. As the horse walked in a circle, the auger turned, carrying the water to the desired destination. Schlickeysen replaced the knives in Speckstruyff's barrel with Archimedes' auger, moved the exit hole from the side to the end of the barrel, and invented the first mechanical vertical auger machine for the extrusion of a column of clay. Now continuous extrusions of clay for making brick and tile were possible. His machine was patented between 1855 and 1860 and proved to be a major industrial breakthrough.[3]

As brick factories were inventing methods to expedite their process, so were the potteries in Europe. The first manual plunger-type extruder was developed in Europe as a way to make coils. This dod, pug, or wad box was used predominately by English potteries in the 1700s and utilized a plunger forced down the barrel by a turning corkscrew handle located at the top of the tool.

Early potters didn't use kiln shelves so they fired their pots in saggers and loaded them in the kiln using a boxing technique. Here the saggers were put together rim to rim and foot to foot in the kiln, creating tall stacks. Great quantities of spaghetti-like strips of clay were placed between the saggers to ensure a distribution of weight to keep the stacks

Barbara Brown, Vase Form, 11" x 4½" x 2", 2000. Altered extrusion using the square hollow die, fired to cone 10 oxidation. Photo by Wilson Grahm.

Jean Latka, Footed Bowl, 12" x 9" x 4", 1994. Lip formed from extruded strips using the handle die and placed into a plaster mold. Feet added when the form has dried to the leather-hard stage, fired to cone 10 reduction.

Jean Latka, Baskets, 18" x 9", 1995. Extruded porcelain handle using the hollow die and manipulated to fit thrown pot, reduction cone 10.

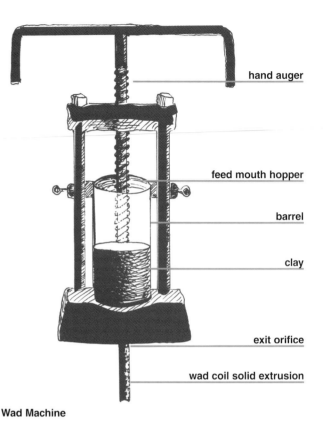

hand auger

feed mouth hopper

barrel

clay

exit orifice

wad coil solid extrusion

Wad Machine

straight and to prevent the pots from sticking together during firing. These strips were called wads and the wad machine was located next to the kiln.[4]

The first pugmills were called piston or box presses and were built around 1828. For the first time, production of thin-walled products such as hollow bricks and drainpipes was possible. The world was changing quickly and it wasn't long afterwards that a continually operating, vertical pugmill with interchangeable dies was patented. Ceramic extrusion, as we know it today, was born.

It was in Europe during the 1950s that the extruder made its introduction into the world of ceramic arts. Two prominent artists, Antoni Cumella of Spain and Allessio Tasca of Italy, created bodies of work which demonstrated the vast sculptural forms that extruded work could embrace. In 1963 Cumella designed a large mural for the Spanish Pavilion of the New York World's Fair which was composed of 104 extruded pieces, each 36" x 20".

Alessio Tasca held an exhibition in 1967 that demonstrated the powerful influence of the extruder in his work, creating a body of work that ranged from tableware to large sculptures.

Across the Channel, Englishman Oliver Bulley was also exploring the possibilities of the extruder and began marketing a device he called the Clay Bulley, which was a manual extruder. At the same time U.S. potter Al Johnsen patented his first Super Duper Clay Extruder and Ted Randall built one for his own personal use. It was the early 1970s and these potters were searching for a faster way to make handles for teapots, casseroles, and mugs and found their solutions through extrusion. The extruder had found its place in the ceramic arts and since then the extruder's uses have become as diverse and varied as the artists who use them.

Sources:

1. Alfred B. Searle, *The Pottery Gazette and Glass Trade Review Offices*, London, England, 1920.
2. Willi Bender, "From Craftsmanship to Industry - The Development of Brick-Making Technology in the 19th Century," *Tile and Brick International*, Volume 12, No. 1, 1996.
3. Willi Bender, same as above, Volume 2, No. 2, 1996.
4. Harry Davis, *The Potter's Alternative*, Chapter 7, Chilton Book Co., Radnor, PA, 1987.

Chapter 2
What Is an Extruder?

Many well equipped clay studios and classrooms have an extruder and use it in some capacity. Considering the contributions an extruder can make to your clay constructing methods, it is a worthwhile investment.

As with any new piece of equipment, learning how to operate it to its fullest extent takes a certain amount of experimentation and time. Every clay artist who successfully integrates extrusions into their work feels it to be an indispensable piece of equipment and a springboard for creative ideas.

Ceramic extrusion is the method of giving shape to clay by forcing it through a die. The extruder is a machine that consists of a barrel, an auger or plunger plate, and a die located on the end of the barrel. When clay is put into the barrel via the hopper mouth and forced out the end through the die, the clay takes the three-dimensional shape of that die.

In the most expansive definition of a manual extruder, a wire loop with a handle, pulled through clay, could be called an extruder. Utilized extensively throughout Europe, this tool is a variation on a simple wire trimming tool. The loop is pulled through a block of clay and the resulting shape is that of the loop.

There are two distinctly different kinds of clay extruders: the plunger type and the pugmill type. The plunger-type is similar in design to a caulking gun. Here a plate is encased in the barrel and when clay is fed into the hopper mouth, the pressure from the lever pushes against the plunger plate, forcing the clay down the length of the barrel and out an opening at the end.

Plunger-type extruders can be powered pneumatically, hydraulically, or manually, with pneumatic and manual being the most common. The pneumatic powered extruder requires an air compressor that will deliver an air supply of 70 to 100 psi. The air flow is controlled by a foot pedal. Stepping on the pedal sends air to push the plunger plate against the clay in the barrel and out the die. The advantage of using a pneumatic powered extruder is that both hands, when not feeding the clay into the hopper mouth, are free to control and work with the extrusion.

Manual plunger-type extruders are hand powered and operated by pushing down on a lever designed to provide maximum leverage and force. With a barrel limited to 6" in

> "To my way of thinking the prime function of the extruder is to save labor and through the labor saving aspect of the process there has been created a new kind of aesthetic related to the mechanistic nature of extrusions. The extruder is a tool, albeit a great tool, but still a tool and like any tool, the objects created are only as interesting as the mind and heart that creates them."
>
> *Jack Sures*

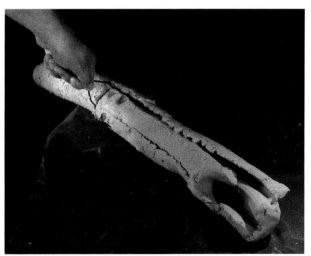

A wire tool being pulled through clay.

diameter and the potential to hold up to ten pounds of clay, manual extruders are ideal for extruding small to medium size extrusions.

There are a variety of small manual extruders on the market today that provide limited yet interesting textural extrusions. A miniature finger extruder is similar to a garlic press in size and operation. The clay is put into a small barrel and a plunger closes over it. Pushing down on the lever sends the clay through tiny dies to create string-like extrusions. Also readily available are small, hand-operated extruders that are the same size and work on the same prin-

Bailey hand extruder.

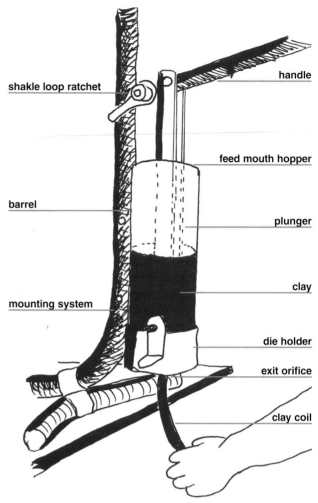

shakle loop ratchet

barrel

mounting system

handle

feed mouth hopper

plunger

clay

die holder

exit orifice

clay coil

Manual Plunger Extruder

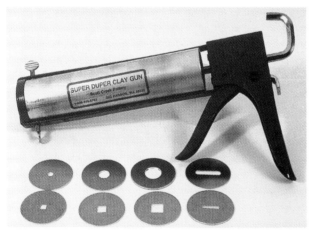

The Super Duper Clay Gun. Photo courtesy of Scott Creek Pottery.

"The great challenge of the extruder today lies in the designing for this new tool. Once you get over the thrill of extruding all your handles or coils in ten seconds flat, you may easily settle for making some fast and simple products. Extrude a tube, attach a bottom, squeeze the top, and get a vase. Many potters will want to stop there. The hard part lies in trying *not* to imitate thrown or slab forms. The aim should be rather to create something special that cannot be done better another way, that is by casting, jiggering, or even throwing.

One suggestion I would offer is to stop designing things vertically as they are produced from the wheel but to start thinking horizontally from the cross section."

Michael Cohen

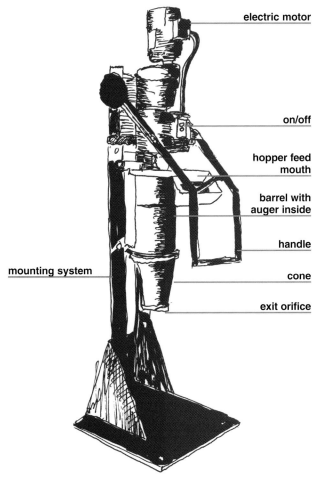

- electric motor
- on/off
- hopper feed
- mouth
- barrel with auger inside
- handle
- mounting system
- cone
- exit orifice

Pugmill Extruder

The exposed auger of the Flying Hybird Ex.

"The extruder is a tool - a valuable and challenging one. As it has been with any tool, the discovery of possibilities for creative design rests in the resourceful minds and hands of each of us."

John Glick

ciple as a caulking gun. Because their barrel is larger than a miniature extruder, they can produce longer, more continuous extrusions.

Manual extruders are really designed to extrude simple shapes such as handles, decorations, small sculptural forms, and additions such as lips and pedestals for pots.

In contrast, the pugmill extruder is a pugmill that has been adapted to also function as an extruder. A pugmill is machine that has an auger encased in a barrel, similar to a meat grinder. Welded to the auger shaft are blades that assist in mixing the clay. The auger rotates and turns in the barrel, homogenizing and mixing the clay as it passes down the

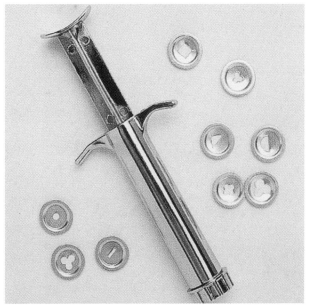

The Kemper Finger Klay Gun. Photo courtesy of Kemper Tools.

The Gladstone Horizontal Pugmill Extruder. Photo courtesy of Gladstone Engineering.

A heavy-duty pugmill and tile extruder. Photo courtesy of Bluebird Manufacturing.

Jean Latka with the "Flying Hybird" extruder. This is a vertical pugmill with a 9" expansion box that allows for longer and wider extrusions.

Alessio Tasca, Terragno, 4' x 4' x 4', 1997, carved from a large extrusion using red and brown clay, oxidation cone 10. Photo by the artist.

"It is important to find a well-made extruder that is adaptable to your needs. As with the wheel, however, once you learn how to use it, what are you going to make? After mastering centrifugal force and friction perhaps it's now time to use gravity and inertia to make a personal statement. Like throwing, it only looks easy."

Michael Cohen

length of the barrel before exiting out the tapered end. When clay is forced down the barrel it is necessary to compress it and this is accomplished by tapering the end or adding a cone-shaped attachment to the end.

Operated primarily by electricity, pugmills come in a variety of sizes and are rated by the amount of clay they can pug per hour. A standard studio pugmill will pug between 400 to 2,400 pounds of clay per hour, while industrial ones can pug up to 14,000 pounds per hour. Pugged clay has been homogenized. For the studio potter, pugging clay replaces the traditional wedging of clay, which is the final prepara-

Brick being made at Gladding McBean from a giant pugmill.

> "The beauty of mundane, repetitive work is that one can and must daydream in the process of doing the work. Watching all those slugs of clay sliding out of the pugmill, thinking of the day's forms and dreaming of ones to come, the mind takes a turn and asks, 'What if?' At that point the floodgates open and out pours the river of endless possibilities."
>
> *Jean Latka*

Jean Latka, Basket, 14" x 12" x 12", 1996, handles extruded using the hollow die and attached to a wheel-thrown form, fired to cone 03.

tion step before sitting down to the potter's wheel.

Some pugmills offer an optional die-airing apparatus. De-airing clay is a way to increase its plasticity by removing air cavities, bringing clay particles into closer contact with each other.

The barrel of the pugmill can be made from steel, aluminum, or stainless steel, with the latter two being superior because they inhibit rust in the barrel. The shaft of the auger is constructed from stainless steel for durability.

Extrusions are limited in size to the diameter of the barrel. If the barrel exit is 3" in diameter, the attached die can be no larger than 3". Gladding McBean, a ceramic pipe production plant in Lincoln, California, uses a pugmill with a barrel 6 feet in diameter to make sewer pipe. The majority of clay studios, though, don't require such giant pieces of equipment. To extrude larger pieces without increasing the size of the barrel, they add an expansion box to the end of the barrel. This box, usually about 10" in diameter and 2" thick, fills with clay and when the die is attached to it, has the potential of extruding forms 10" wide.

Nils Lou, Teapots, 10" x 6" x 6", 1989, extruded and altered forms, fired to cone 10 in an anagama kiln. Photo by the artist.

Plunger or Pugmill?
Which Is Right for You?

The difference between the manual plunger and the pug-

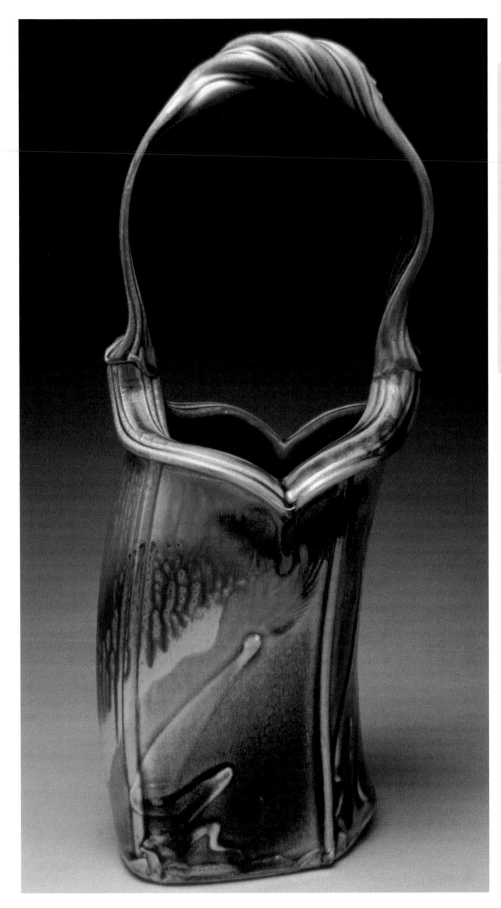

"When using the extruder I am extremely conscious of the mechanical nature of the process. All of my extrusions are altered by either stretching, twisting, or rolling, to give them an organic quality that complements my thrown forms."

Steven Hill

Steven Hill, Extruded Basket, 18" x 18" x 6", 1991, extruded body, rim, and handle, multiple glazes, single fired to cone 10. Photo by Al Surratt.

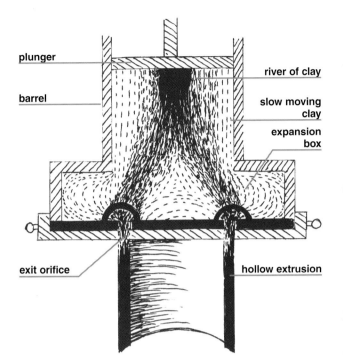

plunger

barrel

river of clay

slow moving clay

expansion box

exit orifice

hollow extrusion

This die has many holes. The longer strips in the center demonstrate how the clay moves faster in the middle.

Studio Pugmill 425, the type we use in our studio, mounted on the wall vertically. Photo courtesy of Bluebird Manufacturing.

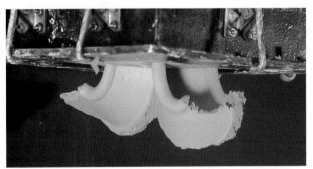

Clay coming out of an X-shaped die. The center clay shears apart from the slower moving clay coming out the sides.

A baffle mounted in the center of the X-shaped die to slow the clay coming out the center.

mill extruder is the size of the extrusions they produce. With a pugmill extruder, an expansion box can be incorporated, thus expanding the extruding capabilities. It's also easier to change clays using a pugmill extruder because the clay runs through the barrel quickly.

Changing dies on any extruder, manual or powered, can be simple and easy if a "quick release" system has been incorporated. These systems utilize quick release fasteners that are attached to the extruder and are very handy additions which surpass the traditional C-clamp method of holding the dies in place. As with the plunger-type extruder, the pugmill must have a die mounting system that accommodates the use of commercial and custom dies.

The main advantage of the manual plunger extruder is that it is manually operated so there's no danger of the motor breaking down. Made of durable metal, manual extruders

Anne E. Hirondelle, Mume Diptych, 15" x 27" x 9", 1989, oxidation cone 10. "I use extrusions in virtually every form I make. Both the linear qualities and the negative spaces that I am able to achieve with the addition of extruded elements are basic to my way of seeing." Photo by the artist.

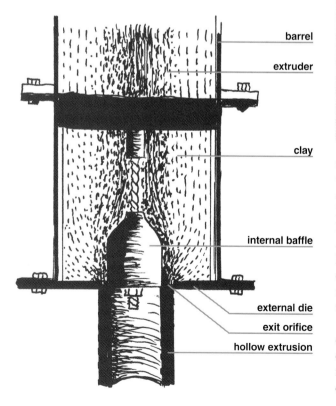

barrel

extruder

clay

internal baffle

external die

exit orifice

hollow extrusion

"I use extrusions in virtually every form I make. Both the linear qualities and the negative spaces I am able to achieve with the addition of extruded elements and are basic to my way of seeing."

Anne Hirondelle

are easy to maintain and repairs usually consist of a simple weld should any seams tear under pressure. Manual extruders are well designed and the placement of the lever ensures little stress to the back and arms of the operator. They are lightweight enough to be easily mounted to tables or walls. A wide variety of commercial dies, often sold in packets or kits, are available, but custom dies will also fit most manual extruders. Each commercial manual extruder has its own die mounting system located at the end of the barrel that holds the dies in place during the extrusion process.

There are only a few disadvantages of the manual extruder. The barrel is small, so the size of the extrusions are limited to that size. An expansion box can be added but doing so necessitates the use of additional physical force to push the clay through the expansion box and out the die. Manual

David Hendley, Pitcher, 12" x 6" x 6", 1989, wood-fired stoneware. "The pitcher is wheel thrown, but both the 'rope' top and the handle were made from extrusions that were manipulated after extruding." Photo by the artist.

extruders are only as fast as the individual feeding and working the lever. Consequently, we find them slow for mass production needs. The only other problem we have experienced is that occasionally, when feeding clay into the hopper mouth, air is trapped in the clay, causing blowouts in the extrusion.

The pugmill extruder's main advantage is that it is powered by an electric motor. It can do everything the manual plunger extruder does with the added benefit of pugging the clay. For extrusion capabilities, the pugmill is superior to the manual extruder. Because the clay is forced under mechanical pressure down the barrel, the extrusions can be larger and more complex in design. The automated feature, partnered with an expansion box, offers the capability to extrude wider, longer, and more complex extrusions, including all hollow and asymmetrical shapes and large cylinders that can be made into slabs.

The major disadvantage of pugmills is size and weight. Pugmills are heavy and awkward to move around. If used horizontally they require a table, which takes up valuable floor space. Horizontal extrusions have a tendency to collapse and have to be supported as they exit the machine unless the clay is very stiff. If the pugmill is to be mounted vertically, a substantial wall or column is required.

When either the manual extruder or the pugmill extruder has not been in use for an extended period of time, the clay hardens and it is necessary to clean the machine. This becomes a rather laborious chore, especially with the pugmill because the nuts and bolts have to be taken out to remove the barrel every time which, due to its weight, is bulky and heavy.

Manual extruders are considerably less expensive than pugmills.

The Theory of Extrusion

Clay is a material that works well when extruded. The clay matrix is such that the particles align and adhere to themselves as they are compressed through the die plate. When force is exerted correctly and evenly, extrusions exhibit structural integrity in the wet, dry, and fired states.

In an effort to understand the movement of the clay through the barrel, it is helpful to visualize the clay as being similar to water in a river. The water moves fastest in the middle of the river; as it spreads out towards the banks, the speed and force decrease. This is due to a diffusion of energy that moves from the center outward. Plus there is

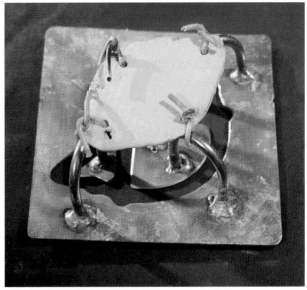

The external baffle is attached directly to this die.

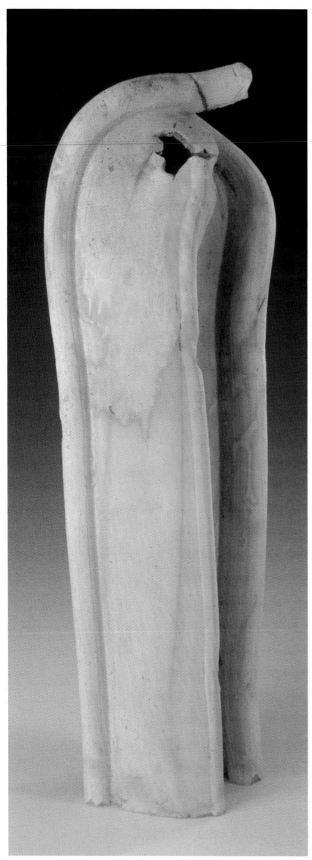

Kaolyn Rose, Grace, 18" x 6" x 6", 1979, salt bisque fired, cone 010. Photo by the artist.

greater resistance along the river banks, thus causing drag on the water. So it is with the extruder. The clay forced down the middle of the barrel moves at a faster rate than the clay on the sides.

The clay moves the fastest out the center of the die and slower down the sides. The interface between the fast and slow moving clay is called laminar flow. This disparity of movement between the two clays will often cause them to shear apart.

One solution to this problem is to slow the movement of the center clay. Many commercial companies will incorporate an internal baffle into the pugmill for this purpose. A baffle is a block of wood or metal that can be attached either to the die or can be permanently installed inside the barrel. It's function is to slow the flow of the clay as it travels down the center of the barrel. When the clay comes into contact with the baffle, it is redirected to the sides of the barrel and then through the die to produce a more even extrusion with less tearing.

Four factors govern the flow of clay out of the extruder: 1) clay consistency, 2) size and shape of the die hole, 3) location of the hole on the die plate, and 4) the force available to push the clay down the barrel and out the die. All these factors need to be considered for optimal extrusion capabilities.

Clay Consistency

The consistency of the clay is the first factor governing the flow of an extrusion. A wet, soft clay is easier to extrude than a dry, hard clay. A smooth plastic clay is less likely to tear as it exits and will conform best to a complicated and detailed die. The drawback to using a wet, plastic clay is that it shrinks and distorts as it dries, which contributes to cracking. It is best to use clay of a medium consistency which has from 6% to 10% fine grog (60-mesh) or other nonshrinking materials in the clay body. The plastic content (ball clay) should equal about one third of all the ingredients.

Commercial brick factories, in an effort to reduce product variability and control losses, extrude a leather-hard clay that has about 8% to 14% water content. This produces a brick that exhibits little change between the initial production to the final firing.

Bill St. John, "The Bubble", 6" x 3" x 3", 1972, hollow extrusion dowel rolled inside to give organic shape, raku fired, cone 010. Photo by the artist.

Dies offset from center produce uneven pressure and create a curved shape.

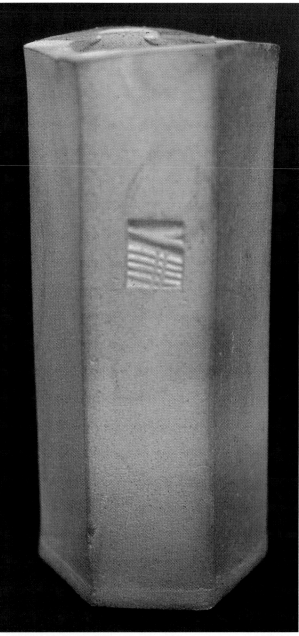

D. Durant, Cylinder, 18" x 6" x 6", 1984, stoneware wood fired, cone 10 reduction. Photo by the artist.

Size and Shape of the Die Hole

The shape and size of the hole in the die plate will directly effect the flow of the extrusion. The barrel size of the extruder must be in proportion to the size of the die opening. A die with a small opening cannot be used on a large diameter barrel because the pressure of a large amount of clay would be too great for the small opening. Because the clay cannot exit fast enough through the opening, the die would become deformed or ruined completely unless constructed from a strong material.

The opposite happens if the die hole is too large. The extrusion undergoes no compression as it exits the die and the clay fails to take the shape of the die.

Some clay artists have a number of extruders in their studios of various sizes, enabling them to extrude any shape, any size, on a correctly proportioned extruder.

Location of the Hole on the Die Plate

The location of the hole on the die plate is critical for the clay to have an even flow. Differential pressure is a term used to describe a gradual distribution of energy. A simple hole located in the center of the die is the easiest form to extrude because the clay moves at a uniform rate with the least amount of resistance.

When the hole is placed off-center, the flow of clay is redirected because uneven pressure is being exerted on the die. The clay passes through the die at different rates, giving the extrusion a curved shape. This can be used as an advantage with forms such as a curved bowl.

Force to Power the Extrusion

There must be sufficient power to drive the extruder. The volume of clay extruded and the rate that it exits the machine is directly proportional to the size of the barrel and the power driving it.

Manual extruders are dependent on the strength of the person operating the tool. Machine-powered pugmills have an electric motor that turns the auger in predetermined rotations per minute (RPM). Plunger-type extruders are driven either by pneumatic (air) or hydraulic (fluid) pressure or are manually driven.

Though the technical particulars governing extruders might appear complicated, extruding forms is a simple process. Put a chunk of medium soft clay in the hopper, slap on a die with a hole in the center, add a little power, and you are in the world of extrusions.

Candyce Ganahl, Vase, 18" x 9" x 9", 1993, stoneware, fired cone 10 reduction. Photo by the artist.

"Truly creative work is a combination of hand, heart and mind. Skill to put ideas into practice, passion to give the work conviction, and the intellect to infuse a rationale to the course of action."

Bernard Leach

Paul Lewing, Extruded Vase, 4" x 5" x 7½", 1985, porcelain, fired cone 10. Photo by the artist.

Jim Nash, Vase, 18" x 6" x 4", 1992, extruded stoneware fired to cone 01 with reticulating glaze. Photo by the artist.

Tom Latka, ceramic wall mural with sconce lighting created in 1997. 6' x 4' x 6". Commercial tile with hand-built center and extruded coils. From the collection of Pueblo Mortgage.

Tom Latka, Sculpture "Brothers" created in 1999. 8" x 6" x 6". Oxidation gray glaze fired to cone 01. Extruded forms curved as they came out of the extruder.

Chapter 3
Clay Bodies for Extrusions

There are many commercial clays suitable for extruding. Clays purchased from a distributor have been premixed at a factory using a formula that the company has either developed or purchased from a clay artist. You also have the option of creating your own clay formula.

Whether you mix your own clay or buy it premixed, the clay's journey from the field to your worktable is basically the same and deserves a few words.

Clay Sources and Types

All clays are divided into two groups: residual and sedimentary. Residual clays are those that remained near the source of the original rock formation. Because they were not subjected to the erosion process, they have large, coarse-grained particles and are usually nonplastic. Sedimentary clays are those that have been transported by wind and rain away from the original rock formation of their source. During transport, the particles become contaminated with other materials and organic matter, mostly iron oxide, giving them a brown or red color. Sedimentary clay particles are small, so sedimentary clay is more plastic than residual clay.

The clay used by potters and artists in this country comes from clay mines throughout the U.S., Canada, and Mexico. Clay is either dug, mined, power-hosed, or blasted from the earth. Usually, large earth-moving bulldozers excavate huge clay deposits, gather the giant chunks, and haul them off to processing plants where they are crushed, ground, screened, bagged, and shipped to the clay manufacturer.

Raw ingredients, when subjected to forces of weather, will naturally change over time and it is understood that a clay deposit will vary from one end of a mine to the other. Consequently, it is important to test each new shipment of raw materials before it is mixed. A sample is taken from each pallet, mixed with water, and fired in a test kiln. This test is then compared with samples from previous batches to see if they exhibit the same characteristics. If the manufacturer is convinced that consistency has been maintained, the clay is again screened to remove final impurities before being mixed, and the mixed clay is sent to a distributor to be sold.

Fire clay is a sedimentary clay found predominately in coal seams. It is refractory and has a high content of alumina, which makes it ideal for high-fire pottery and ceramics,

"The trick is not to fool with the clay's inherent desire to be expressive. Pay attention to the clay, not only for the sake of each piece, but because the clay will offer - or impose - its own suggestions of new forms and ways to work. The techniques of hand-building take advantage of clay's ability to capture gesture and movement, its power to record processes. I am intrigued by what happens when clay is rolled, stretched, pressed, incised, inlayed, extruded, bent, cut, and put back together."

Hayne Bayless

Extruded pugged clay.

maturing at around 2372°F. Fire clay is commonly used for making hard brick, insulating brick, and kiln furniture. The color ranges from pure white to pale buff after firing, with speckled iron particles evident, which are usually stiff and coarse, making fire clay unsuitable for throwing or extruding.

Kaolin is one of the purest residual clays, containing very little impurity or iron. High in alumina, kaolin fires white and is a major ingredient in porcelain yet has little plasticity. It is a high-fire clay discovered in China in roughly 200 B.C. Kaolin means "high ridge" or "mountain," a reference to where the original deposits were mined.

D. Hayne Bayless, Three Pitchers, 8" x 5" x 4", 1997, porcelain clay with black slip for decoration, fired to cone 10. Photo by the artist.

View of four colored clays at Summit brickyard. Pueblo, Colorado.

Ball clay.

Ball clay is a sedimentary clay similar to kaolin after it has been fired. It is a highly plastic clay and is the basis of many clay bodies. Alone it is too slippery and fine, but used in combination with sand, grog, or fire clay, it becomes highly workable. It is called ball clay because it was transported in balls on the backs of donkeys from the clay pits where it was first mined.

Stoneware clay is medium to high-fire, exhibits good plasticity, and, depending on the atmosphere of the kiln when fired, can be pale buff to dark brown in color.

Earthenware clay is the most abundant in the world, usually found a few feet beneath the surface of the soil. It is a sedimentary clay that has collected debris and organic matter for eons before becoming lodged in the strata beneath a lake or river. Earthenware clay has a low firing temperature, rich color, and a porous body, making it ideal for building purposes, cooking vessels, and water containers.

Bentonite clay formed in the prehistoric ages from the airborne dust of volcanic eruptions. It has the finest particle size of any clay and yet expands and shrinks dramatically, up to 40 times its size. Composed predominately of silica, bentonite is used as an additive to a clay body as a plasticizer.

Mixing Your Own Clay

Rarely is it possible to find a clay body existing naturally in the world that is completely acceptable. Usually it will not be plastic enough or will contain too much flux to fire to a high temperature. Or it may exhibit an undesirable texture or color. Therefore, to make a versatile, good working body with specific desired characteristics, many artists formulate their own clay bodies.

A good extruding clay body will exhibit many of the same characteristics as a good throwing body: plasticity,

John Stephenson, Curve Anxiety, 43" x 77½" x 1¾", 1992. Mural created from extruded slabs. Photo by the artist.

moderate shrinkage, desirable firing temperature, and a minimal amount of cracking and warping.

Extruding, like throwing or hand-building, can be achieved using any clay body as long as there is enough ball clay or bentonite in the clay to provide a soft, pliable extrusion.

Plasticity is essential for extruding. To determine if a clay body is sufficiently plastic, roll out a coil of clay and bend it in a circle around your finger. If the coil cracks and breaks, the clay is not plastic enough and will require additions of plasticizing ingredients. To make a clay more plastic you can:

- ◆ add more ball clay
- ◆ omit or reduce the grog or use a 200-400 mesh grog
- ◆ add bentonite which has been slaked down in water
- ◆ add more water, making a wetter, more pliable clay
- ◆ use a clay body high in stoneware or porcelain clays and low in fire clay
- ◆ use a clay that has been aged long enough to allow the individual particles to absorb more water, making the clay more workable.

Many clay manufacturers will custom mix an artist's clay formula, providing the ease of ready-made clay without the work of having to mix it. The problem with most

> "Clay is a responsive material. Apply pressure and it compresses. Release the pressure and it expands. Reacting to compression and release, clay seems almost alive, to breathe. Most of us experience this at the potter's wheel and it is very noticeable when using the extruder. Extruded forms can be very expressive. They are as three-dimensional recordings of expansion and compression in the clay."
>
> *John Stephenson*

premixed clays is that they are de-aired, very hard, and unsuitable for extruding. Before using hard clay, it is necessary to pug it with additional water to soften it and make it ready to extrude. If you plan to have a clay company formulate and mix your clay body, stipulate a minimum water content of 27%.

Clay Body Formulas

The following clay body formulas have proven to be successful for extruding. As with any new recipe, make a sample batch and experiment with it before mixing large quantities.

Rina Peleg, Earth Structure, 5' x 6' x 3'6", 1983, extruded coils assembled in basket form on site and fired to cone 6. Photo by the artist.

Stoneware

Stoneware bodies are made from stoneware clays and become vitrified at around 2370°F. They often have a percentage of fire clay, sand, or grog to give an open texture to the clay and to reduce shrinkage and warping. Stoneware clay is typically associated with hand-crafted pottery because the clay matures at the same temperature as the glaze, forming an integrated body/glaze bond.

Latka's Stoneware Body, Cone 10
for throwing, extruding, sculpting

Cherokee fire clay 10%
Cedar Heights Goldart fire clay 10%
Hawthorn fire clay 30%
Lincoln fire clay 20%
Silica 3%
Kaolin 10%
Ball clay 10%
Grog (400-mesh) 4%
Feldspar 4%

Porcelain

Porcelain bodies are compounded primarily from kaolin, silica, and feldspar. Porcelain is very similar to stoneware yet is free of the impurities, resulting in a white to off-white body when fired. A characteristic of porcelain is fine texture and extreme plasticity, which enable the clay

Terry Riley, Godzilla, 24" x 6" x 6", 1978, extruded stoneware vase with thrown top, fired to cone 10. Photo by the artist.

Lyn Bond, Clay Baskets, 1999, low-fired earthenware and majolica accent and Mason stains, fired to cone 06. Photo by Daren Maranya.

Jean Latka, Drape Plate, 8" x 8" x 2", 1985, low-fired earthenware with majolica glaze and Mason stains, fired to cone 01.

to be worked thinly, giving a translucent quality to the piece when fired.

Rina Peleg's White Porcelain Body, Cone 6, Oxidation or Reduction

Talc	3.9%
Custer feldspar	11.5%
Nepheline syenite	9.6%
Ball clay	5.8%
Georgia kaolin	17.3%
Kaolin (6 tile clay)	34%
Silica	17.3%

Tom Latka, Bowl, 14" x 16" x 6", 1987, extruded straps placed in mold to harden, thrown lip accent added, fired to cone 10.

Earthenware

Earthenware clays are the most common and most used clays because they mature at such a low temperature - from cone 010 to cone 01. Also called terracotta, earthenware is a porous clay, characteristically red and orange in color because of the high concentration of iron oxide, which also acts as a flux.

Jeanie Briggs' Red Clay, Cone 04, Oxidation or Reduction

Talc	10%
Cedar Heights Goldart clay	20%
Cedar Heights Redart clay	60%
Fire clay	10%

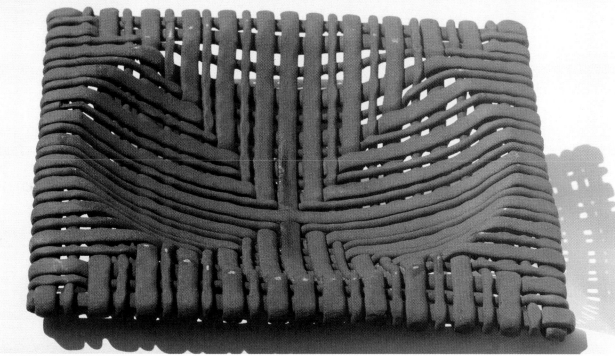

Gary Skul, Square Bowl, 18" x 18" x 2", 1995, stoneware extruded coils, draped into form and slightly flattened, fired to cone 6. Photo by the artist.

Tom Morrissey's Extruding Clay Body, Cone 8 to 10

Cedar Heights Goldar 23%
Cedar Heights Redart. 23%
Lincoln fire clay 43%
Sand (100-mesh) 8%
Vermiculite 2%

Paris Black Clay Body, Cone 4, Oxidation or Reduction

Barnard slip 13.3%
Earthenware clay 13.4%
Ocmulgee red clay 13.3%
PBX fire clay or any plastic fire clay 40%
Wollastonite. 20%

Add
Black iron oxide 4
Iron chromate 4
Manganese dioxide 10

Horizon Gold Yellow Clay Body, Cone 4, Oxidation

Cedar Heights Goldart clay 34%
A.P. Green fire clay 15%
Pine Lake fire clay. 45%
Wollastonite 3.75%

Add
Macaloid. 2

Jean Latka, Molded Bowl, 14" x 6" x 3", 1995, extruded straps draped into mold, fired to cone 10. Photo by the artist.

Extruding Kiln Furniture

Extruding kiln furniture can be challenging because there is little plasticity in the body. Nevertheless, the extrusions are not very long and can exit the machine in one piece without breaking. With kiln furniture it's important to have consistent dimensions for the various pieces.

Terry Riley's Kiln Furniture Body, Cone 10

XX sagger clay 25%
Kaolin 25%
Porcelain or stoneware grog (30-mesh) 50%

Chapter 4
Dies - Theory and Construction

Learning how to construct your own dies will enable you to develop and create forms that are not available from a commercial die maker, giving your work a truly unique look and allowing you to create exactly the piece you envision.

The key to constructing a good working die is to remember the basic premise that clay is a viscous material which, when subjected to pressure, can be made to flow like a river. The middle of the river, like the clay in the center of the pugmill, flows the fastest. This is because there is more friction along the sides of the barrel, putting drag on the clay and slowing it down. The clay in the center receives a greater proportion of the force, has less friction, and consequently moves at a faster rate through the machine. Designing, constructing, and extruding from a die is a trial and error process that requires experimentation blended with a certain amount of intuition.

There are two ways extrusions exit the machine: through a simple solid die shape or through a more complicated hollow die shape. Extrusions, both solid and hollow, can be symmetrical or asymmetrical.

The solid shape is made with one hole in the die. The clay fills the hole in the die and comes out in a solid mass. The most common applications of the solid die are coils and bricks. With the hollow die, the flow of clay is impeded by adding a solid center in the die hole. The clay is forced into the space between an inner and outer plate and a hollow core shape is the result.

Solid centers in the die holes force the clay between the inner and outer plates, creating a hollow core in the extruded form.

"I have used the smaller diameter extruded tubing to make a trophy horn for a musical contest and it could be blown like a brass instrument. This size tubing, closed at one end, also made interesting hanging chimes as well as bars for a xylophone-type instrument."

Nancy Hall

A solid coil die shape.

A hollow die shape.

One type of hollow die is called a bridge die. In this type of hollow die, the inner and outer plates are connected by sturdy pieces of metal called bridges. Bridge dies are the best and most commonly used method to make hollow extrusions. They are used by both the ceramic industry and studio artists.

Once the clay has passed over the bridge, it reconnects to itself, creating an intact hollow extrusion. Each extrusion shape requires a specific bridge die that is made to extrude that particular shape.

Another type of hollow die requires two separate pieces for the inner and outer plate which are independent of each other. The inner plate of the die is bolted at the end of the extruder barrel, in the center. The outer plate is attached separately to the end of the extruder. The problem with this type of hollow die is that the inner die plate has to match up perfectly with the outer die plate to get an even thickness in the walls of the extrusion. Because of this difficulty, this type of die is much less common in studios.

The development of the hollow die had a profound effect on industrial ceramics because hollow objects are lighter

Dies for an industrial pugmill extruder.

U bolt metal "bridges" connect the inner and outer plates of the hollow die.

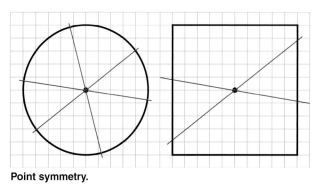

Point symmetry.

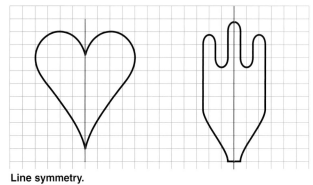

Line symmetry.

weight and use less clay material. Hollow dies also dramatically expanded the repertoire of shapes that could be extruded. Seamless sewer tiles, flue liners, hollow bricks, drain pipes, and screen tiles are the most common applications of the hollow die. The ceramic world uses hollow extruded stilts in the kiln to support kiln shelves.

For the studio clay artist, the hollow die offers the possibility of extruding functional objects such as vases, planters, and lamps as well as providing a springboard to create a variety of sculptural elements and forms.

Die Design Theory

Extrusions can be shaped with either symmetrical or asymmetrical dies. It is important to remember that it easier to extrude with symmetrical dies.

There are two types of symmetry: point symmetry and line symmetry. Point symmetry exists when any line can be drawn anywhere through the center of a shape. Point symmetry is not the same as mirror image, but a direct replica of the other half. Point symmetrical dies are the most common and easy to construct. Simply keep the design in the center of the die.

Line symmetry exists when an object has an exact correspondence of form on opposite sides of a dividing line. In other words, if you cut an object down the middle and fold it over so that the two sides are a perfect match, you have a mirror image on each side. So it is with dies and the extrusions they make. A coil, brick, and cylinder all exhibit symmetrical properties and this is the form primarily used in the clay industry.

Most line symmetrical dies like the rectangle of a brick are centered, but some are constructed with the bulk of the extrusion located away from the center of the die so the clay will flow evenly. This works because the clay in the center of the barrel moves faster than the clay off-center. The larg-

A symmetrical die.

An asymmetrical die that is point symmetrical.

Jean Latka, Blue Platter, 18" x 18" x 2", cone 10, stoneware, fire reduction, handle extrusions.

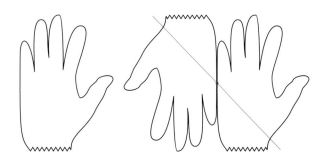

Asymmetircal object.   Point symmetrical object.

"My extrusion fantasy began because I wanted a temple in my yard. Since real temples were too expensive I developed a column-extruding machine that extruded 10" diameter columns to make my own. So we built a little temple out of these columns and sent photographs of it to one of the shelter magazines. They published the photograph as a new product and I got 800 inquiries. I was in the temple business."

Bennett Bean

er off-center opening forces the fastest moving clay to the outer regions nearer the wall of the barrel so that the clay will feed into the bulk of the die at a more even rate.

A shape is asymmetrical if the corresponding edges don't match when the shape is cut down the middle and folded over. The two halves can be moderately or radically different from each other. Asymmetrical dies are used primarily by clay artists who want to create unusual sculptural details and odd, abstract extrusions.

The ultimate goal when designing an asymmetrical die is to make it point symmetrical. First draw a shape, then draw an exact image of it. Turn one of the shapes 180° and match up the sides. Now it is possible to draw a line down the axis through the center at any point. It is now point symmetrical.

The die pictured is an asymmetrical design, point symmetrical, and centered. Once the extrusion is out of the die it can be cut lengthwise to get to the asymmetrical shape originally desired.

When constructing your own dies you can make either symmetrical or asymmetrical dies. The most obvious application and the easiest to construct are solid, symmetrical dies.

Many individuals don't have the time, desire, or equipment to construct their own dies. This is not a problem since there are many commercial extruding companies that offer a large selection of dies from which to choose.

Bennet Bean, Table Base, 2.5', 1991, assembled extruded clay sections, fired to 10. Photo by the artist.

Commercial dies are constructed from different materials. High density plastic, ¾" plywood, steel, aluminum, and stainless steel are the most typical die materials and each has proven to be durable for extruding solid shapes. Aluminum, high density plastic, and stainless steel are superior construction materials because they won't rust.

Commercially available shapes for solid extrusions are fairly typical - round, square, octagonal, cloverleaf, and hexagonal, to name a few. Each shape comes in an assortment of sizes ranging from ¹⁄₁₆" to 4". For smaller extrusions, ¼" to 1" coils for example, some companies put many die holes on one die plate. This makes extruding a large quantity go much quicker, plus manipulating extrusions when they are grouped can create some interesting effects.

The variety of shapes for hollow commercial dies is not as extensive as for solid dies but there is a good selection to get you started. Hollow dies are made from either aluminum, steel, stainless steel, or birch plywood (the cabinetmaker's plywood). In our studio we use aluminum and a

"My work is a response to observing the rhythms and cycles of the natural world around me. From the shorter rhythms of seasons to the almost timeless cycles of stones and mountains, I find endless shapes, textures, and fragments that echo the process of life, death, and rebirth. I use press molds for deer antlers, stones, and fossils to repeat shapes that form the building blocks for my vessels. Within this framework I seek to express feelings I don't often understand, perhaps longings for strength and beauty or the desire to show painful steps I am trying to master or interpretations of numinous dreams that seem like a gift."

Marian Haigh

Marian Haigh, Antler Bowl, 13" x 13" x 4", antlers from extruded coils pressed into molds and manipulated. Photo by Rick Patrick.

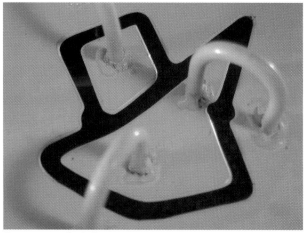

An asymmetrical die.

A Bailey commercial die.

Colin Kellam, Planter, 12" x 10" x 8",1989, reduction cone 10. Photo by the artist.

combination of wood and plastic. The main consideration is that the hollow die must be made from a material strong and durable enough to withstand the pressure from the extruder without breaking.

As with solid dies, commercial hollow die shapes are pretty standard and the collection includes round, square, hexagonal, triangular, rectangular, star-shaped, and clover-leaf-shaped. The sizes range from 1¾" to 9" if an expansion box is incorporated. Experimenting with commercial hollow dies is a perfect way to expand your understanding and working knowledge of dies and the extruder. They will

A variety of dies made from different materials.

familiarize you with extrusion concepts and principles, present you with a variety of challenges which you will learn to resolve, and help you figure out how to incorporate extrusions into your body of work. Once you have navigated through these waters, you will be able to assess the importance the extruder has in your work and decide if you want to expand its role and start designing your own dies.

Constructing a Die

Clay artist Hayne Bayless explains why he prefers to make his own dies. "I have never found a commercially made hollow die that I like. The number of sizes and shapes available is extremely limited, and they produce an extrusion that is much too thick-walled for my purposes. It is preferable to work with extrusions that are no thicker than ⅛". So I make my own dies." Perhaps this is the case with you. You may find that your extruding needs cannot be met on the commercial level. Making your own dies is not a complicated or elaborate procedure and even the clay novice can enjoy designing, fabricating, and using their own designer dies.

All die plates must be constructed from a material that can withstand the force exerted by the extruder. If using wood, we recommend using marine birch plywood because it is made of hardwood with thinner laminations that yield a stronger material yet it is easy to cut and shape.

The materials listed below have been used successfully to construct dies. Each material has its own particular properties and considerations. Consult the list to determine which material will work best for your designer dies. All materials are strong enough when used in the thickness listed on page 42.

Susan Bunzl, Vase, 24" x 16" x 16", 1999, thrown porcelain form with extrusions added. Photo by Kurt Bunzl.

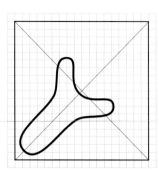

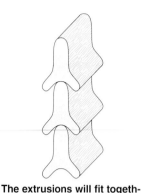

The largest part of the extrusion is located away from the center so the clay will flow evenly.

The extrusions will fit together tongue-and-groove style.

The extrusion produced by the Coil Plus die.

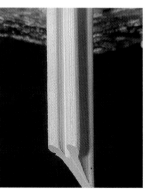

Clay coming through the die.

Die Material	Workability	Longevity
14 gauge steel	fair	excellent
12 gauge stainless steel	fair	excellent
¼" aluminum	good	excellent
⅝" dense plastic	good	good
¾" marine and 7-ply plywood	excellent	fair
¾" marine plywood and ⅛" Plexiglas	good	fair

When designing dies keep in mind that the extruder loves symmetry and functions best when the die hole is centered.

Making a Solid "Coil Plus" Die

This project is a simple, symmetrical solid die not commercially available. This die is the next generation shape for the round coil and is used for hand-building and adding coils to existing forms such as a lip to a thrown vessel.

The shape and principle of this die are similar to that of tongue-and-groove flooring. When the shapes extruded with this die are stacked on top of each other there is more bonding power because more surface area is exposed, making the connections stronger.

1. Cut a piece of ¾" plywood that will fit on the end of your extruder. We used a 6" square piece of wood. Using a ruler, draw a diagonal line from each corner of the plywood. The center of the die is the point where the lines meet.
2. Draw the die shape on graph paper. This is the template for your die. Cut it out and fold it over to make certain it's symmetrical, then trace it onto the plywood. Place the drawing so that the bulk of the extrusion will be closer to the edge of the die.
3. Drill a hole near one edge of your line tracing. Use a drill bit larger than the size of a reciprocating saw blade.
4. Fit the reciprocating saw into the hole and cut along the lines of your shape. If possible, use a metal blade. This blade has the finest teeth and will give a smooth cut.
5. The die will function better if a feed bevel is incorporated into it. This is a beveled edge along the die hole that provides a cleaner extrusion, one with less tearing. The bevel also helps direct the clay into the die. Use a file or router to cut the feed bevel around the hole. Unless a rough surface is desired, make the bevel as smooth as possible. Sand if necessary. Because the extrusion

R. Koop, Carpochino Cups and Saucers, 3½" x 2" x 4", 1997, cup form extruded with slab additions for handles and base, saucers slab formed, majolica glaze colored with Mason stains, fired to cone 03. Photo by Janet Ryan.

from this die will be used explicitly for adding to other coils or pots, we left a rough surface on the area of the die where the extrusion would later be scored for attaching.

6. Now you are ready to mount the die on the end of your extruder. If your extruder has one, use the die mounting system to attach the die. If not, use C-clamps.

7. Load clay into the extruder and extrude the form.

We used this Coil Plus die for a lip on a planter (see page 81).

For a more detailed die, use a combination of ¾" marine plywood (for the support die) and ⅛" Plexiglas (for the master die).

The plywood provides the structural strength while the Plexiglas allows for a more intricate and detailed die since it is easier to cut. Follow the above steps to transfer the extruded image onto the wood and plastic. It's easy to cut the Plexiglas to the shape of the die using a reciprocating saw or coping saw. Sand or file the edges until they are smooth. Using the same reciprocating saw, cut the shape into the plywood, making it just a little bigger than the plastic image. Use commercial glue to join the two surfaces together. To utilize the strength of the plywood, it is important to mount the plastic side of the die facing the extruding clay.

Making a Hollow Die

To make a hollow die, use the same steps as above

Tom Latka, Extrusion or Bust, Cone 1, flash fire. 24" x 18" x 18".

Jim Klingman, Xcups, 6" x 3" x 3", 1999, extruded porcelain clay with foot and handle attached. Photo by the artist.

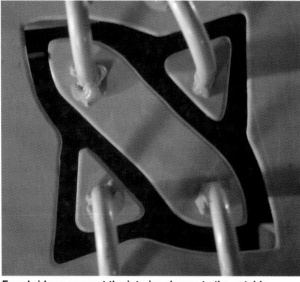

Four bridges connect the interior shapes to the outside shape.

Left: The more intricate shape is in the Plexiglas.

Right: Tom Latka, In and Out, 16" x 10" x 10", formed by putting extrusions in plaster mold, oxidation cone 01.

U bolts bridge the outer and inner forms.

except make two shapes - one for the interior and one for the outside. Make the interior shape smaller than the outside shape and connect them with a bridge.

The majority of our hollow dies are made by a machinist from ¼" aluminum. We have found that this material wears the longest, doesn't rust, and is lighter to handle.

If your hollow die is made of wood, Plexiglas, or dense plastic, use stainless steel U bolts (available at any hardware store) to bridge the two forms together. It's important to use at least three bolts evenly spaced to secure the two dies to one another. It is advisable to attach the bolts with a washer and a minimum of two nuts to each bolt. This will prevent the U bolts from coming loose from the die plate.

There are two ways to weld the steel bridges to steel die plates. Extruder artist Hayne Bayless explains his technique. "Brazing, which is a stronger, higher temperature version of soldering, is the easiest way to connect the pieces together without having to get into welding, which requires more skill and expensive equipment. Small brazing jobs require nothing more than a propane torch and a brazing rod, both found at your local hardware store. Bigger jobs call for MAPP gas which uses the same burner head as the propane bottle but burns hotter."

When experimenting with different shapes to extrude, we make prototypes out of plywood. If the die is one we like and appears promising, we have it made from aluminum.

Tom Latka, Tall Vase, 18" x 4" x 4", 1992, stoneware extruded from cylinder die and altered, fired to cone 10.

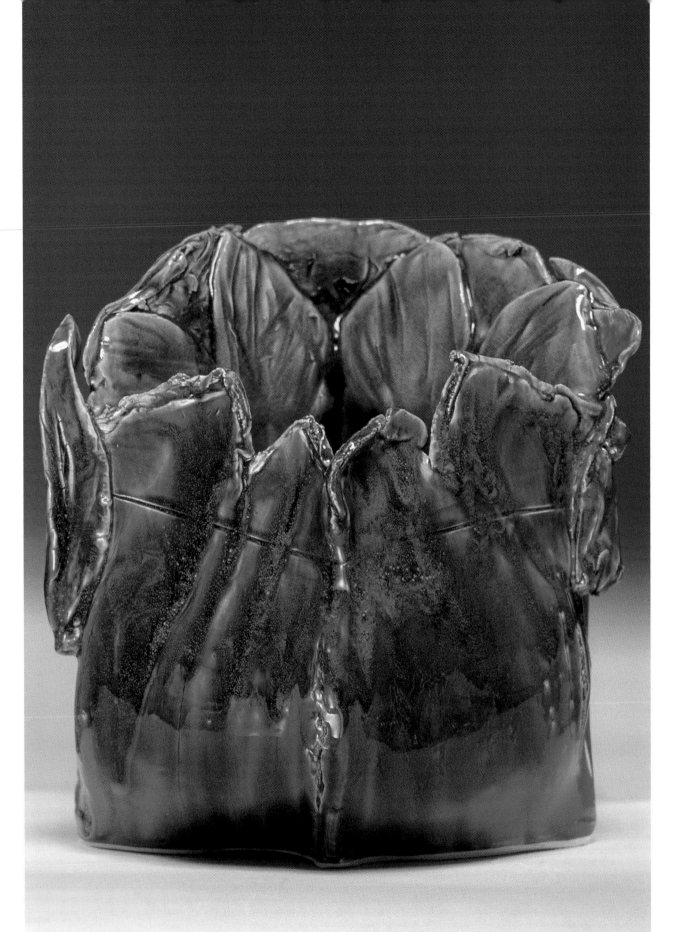

Macy Dorf, Desert Flower, 14" x 18", 1994, extruded and altered clay, using canyon lands as a metaphor, fired to cone 10. Photo by the artist.

Jean Latka, Drape Plate, 12" square, 1996, extruded slab draped over plaster mold and extruded straps added around the edges, stoneware, fired to cone 10.

Walt Schmidt, Pitcher with Straw Glass, pitcher 12" x 6", glass 8" x 3", 1983, extruded stoneware forms with thrown tops. Photo by J. Anthony.

Patrick Crabb, Untitled, 32" x 18" x 18", 1999, wheel-thrown vessel with extruded handle, low fired to cone 02. Photo by the artist.

Chapter 5
Getting Started

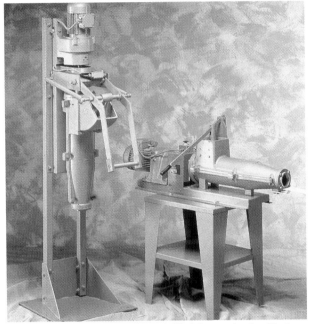

Photo of a vertical and horizontal Gladstone extruder. Photo courtesy of Gladstone Engineering.

"The line is essential, universal, and frugal. I use it as an indicator and also in its capacity as a metaphor for getting from A to B. To travel; to go forth; to journey; be it life's journey or the journey downstairs. A journey one dreads or looks forward to or is simply unaware of. The staircase, the corridor, bridges, the tendrils of a vine, electrical cables and the plumes of a plane are to me all metaphors for journeys.

I am also intrigued by the 'nothing' that surrounds the line. As Lao Tse points out- 'we put 30 spokes together and call it a wheel, but it is the space where there is nothing that the utility of the wheel depends.'"

Isabelle Van Lennep

Equipment and Materials

We live in an automated world. Machines are so integrated into our lives that the thought of existing without them is unfathomable. Ceramics is one of the more labor intensive art forms and the majority of clay artists will concede the need of machinery at some step along the way in the creative process. From mixing the clay to glazing the finished product, chances are a machine of some kind has been used in the process. Machines have the capability to free an artist from the mundane tasks, allowing more time for the imagination to work its wonders.

As with any purchase of studio equipment, certain considerations must be addressed to determine if the machine will be an asset or a detriment. Understanding the initial cost and calculating the length of time it will take to recover that expense is a primary deliberation. Maintenance requirements and life expectancy of the machine are also pertinent considerations, yet one must ultimately ask if the machine will truly contribute to the overall creative process. Will it augment your repertoire or end up being another object stuck off in some corner of the studio?

If we had to rank the importance of the equipment in our studio, number one would be the potter's wheel, followed by the kiln, clay mixer, and pugmill/extruder. The potter's wheel is first because it enabled us to initially entertain the idea of being studio artists and supporting our family through making pottery. The pugmill/extruder ranks in the top four because it opened a new avenue of exploration and creativity that musician Jerry Lee Lewis succinctly says, "shakes my world and rattles my cage."

Originally, we used our pugmill to homogenize the clay used to make the pottery. English potter Harry Davis states, "It is obvious, I think, that of all the mechanical aids, a pugmill offers potters the greatest reward in terms of liberating them to work dedicatedly on the creative and imaginative aspects of their craft." The moment we attached a die to the end of the pugmill, we entered a new realm of creativity where the static implications of the machine fed the unfettered limits of the imagination.

To make extrusions you will need an extruder. Extruders are available at any ceramic supply store (see Sources, page 143, for a list of manufacturers). Your needs (or dreams) will

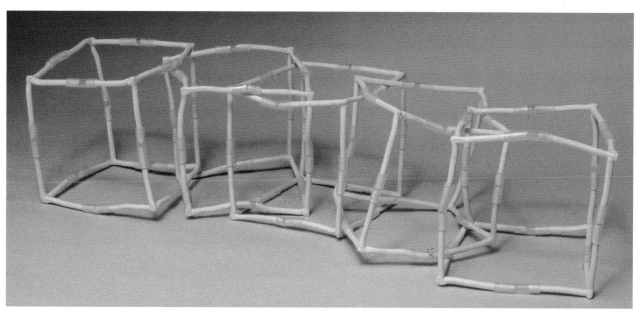

Van Lenner, Untitled, 25" x 5" x 5", 1993, porcelain extrusions constructed with clear rubber tubing, fired to cone 10. Photo by the artist.

Malcolm Wright, Form, 18" x 6" x 6", 1997, extrusion altered and reassembled, fired to cone 10. Photo by Michael Cohen.

"I want to keep my extruded forms as opposites, as a balance to the repeated forms of the wheel. I find that now I am interested in simplifying to the extreme in order to expand the complexity."

Malcolm Wright

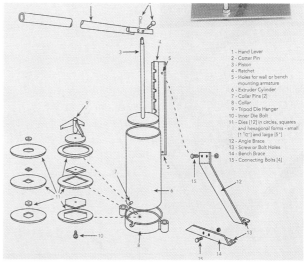

1 - Hand Lever
2 - Cotter Pin
3 - Piston
4 - Ratchet
5 - Holes for wall or bench mounting armature
6 - Extruder Cylinder
7 - Collar Pins [2]
8 - Collar
9 - Tripod Die Hanger
10 - Inner Die Bolt
11 - Dies [12] in circles, squares and hexagonal forms - small (1 1/2") and large (5")
12 - Angle Brace
13 - Screw or Bolt Holes
14 - Bench Brace
15 - Connecting Bolts [4]

A drawing of a Randle plunger-type extruder, showing the different components.

"The fun of working with extruded pieces is the altering of the shapes immediately after the clay is extruded. The more complex the die, the more expandable or contractive is the piece."

Bill Shinn

dictate what kind of extruder to purchase. If you are looking for a tool that will extrude simple forms in small quantities, your best choice is a manually operated plunger type. Many clay artists use this type of extruder with great success.

If you are looking to combine pugging and extruding capabilities in one machine, a studio pugmill is your best option. We have had excellent results with a pugmill to mix and pug clay. By attaching an expansion box to the end of the barrel, the pugmill becomes an extruder.

Installing the Extruder

Install the extruder or pugmill according to the manufacturer's instructions. Due to the weight of a pugmill, if you intend to erect the machine vertically you must attach the pugmill directly to the wall studs, a pillar, or post. If you

Mark Derby, Covered Container, 4" x 16" x 8", 1997, extruded terracotta combined with slab construction, fired to cone 03. "I have come to rely on the extrusion technique for its precision, exactness, and consistency." Photo by the artist.

> "After 30-plus years of working on the wheel, I needed another tool that would relieve the stress on my body and allow me to continue my work producing large clay pieces. The extruder seems to have that potential."
>
> *Macy Dorf*

Steve Bair, Undulation, 36" x 14" x 18", 1987, extruded forms layered in plaster mold, then carved, salt bisque fired to cone 010. Photo by the artist.

have questions about the wall's stability, consult a contractor before mounting the pugmill. There is a great amount of force exerted on an extruder and unless properly mounted, it can literally be pulled from the wall. It must be secured. We constructed a metal frame to which we attached the extruder and then bolted the whole apparatus to a column. Always over build and use the largest lag bolts that will fit through the holes.

When erecting a pugmill or extruder vertically, mount the extruder so that the handle won't be a traffic hazard or obstacle and position the machine so the feed hopper and extrusions are at a comfortable working height yet high enough off the floor to accommodate long extrusions.

When installing a pugmill horizontally on a table or cart, make certain that the tabletop is about 6" lower than what is comfortable. After the extruder is positioned, the table will be at the correct height for working. Mount the extruder to the table using lag screws to securely attach the extruder so it won't move while extruding.

Clay

There are many clay mixtures available today from the ceramic supply store. Each has a special characteristic such as color, firing temperature, and firing method. The moisture content of the clay is an important variable when it comes to extruding. For the best results, use a soft wet clay that will conform readily to the die and flow easily from the machine. On the other hand, brickyards extrude a clay that has only 8% water content and when the extrusions are stacked and wrapped in plastic properly, they can stay moist for up to three years. Store unused clay in plastic bags in a dark corner of the studio.

It's best to start the extruding process using the clay you are familiar with, paying attention to the different aspects of the clay as it goes through the particular phases. Note how it comes out of the extruder, the amount of shrinkage during drying and firing, if warping and cracking are present. Is it

An assortment of tools to use with extrusions.

possible to add appendages and handles without causing cracking? We have developed a clay body that is versatile and we are able to extrude our regular throwing bodies of stoneware, earthenware, and porcelain successfully. Experiment with different clay bodies to find which one suites your tastes and satisfies your design requirements best.

Dies

Commercial dies can be purchased from the same company where you bought your extruder. When you are using the extruder for the first time it is prudent to purchase commercially made dies. Once you become experienced, you will probably want to make your own dies (see page 40 for die-making instructions).

Maintenance

Extruders are practically maintenance free pieces of equipment. The only problem that arises occurs when the clay has been left in the extruder for too long and becomes hard. To prevent this during short periods of time (up to two weeks) when the extruder is not being used, cover the hopper mouth with plastic. Place a wet sponge at the end of the barrel and cover this with plastic also. When the extruder is going to be idle for an extended period of time (more than a month), it is best to dismantle it and remove any clay left in the barrel.

If the clay has dried out, Venco Manufacturing recommends pouring a cup of water into the hopper mouth and letting it set overnight or until the clay softens. Never turn on a studio pugmill until the clay has softened because damage to the coupling may result.

To clean the extruder, remove the barrel and let the clay

dry, then scrape the sides until you've removed all the clay. The auger and shaft will also have clay on them and can be cleaned by using a wire brush and scaper tool. With a hand extruder, lift the plunger out of the barrel and scrape down the sides to remove the dried clay.

Electric extruders, such as pugmills, require periodic cleaning which includes checking the couplings and bearings for wear. For detailed maintenance, consult the manual that comes with the extruder.

Tools and Their Uses

The hand tools used to work and manipulate extrusions are simple, straightforward, and readily available in your studio or kitchen or can be purchased from a pottery supply store. They are listed in order of use as the extrusions exit the extruder.

- ♦ A clean, sturdy worktable to place the extrusions. One that can be accessed from all sides is preferable. Depending on the size of a project, we often set a 4' x 8' sheet of plywood on a table to give us more work surface.
- ♦ A cutting tool. To cut the extrusions from the

Richard, Montgomery, Teapot, 10" x 14" x 5", 1991, extruded forms combined, fired to cone 03. "My discovery of the extruder has proven to be a catalyst in my exploration of the vessel form." Photo by the artist.

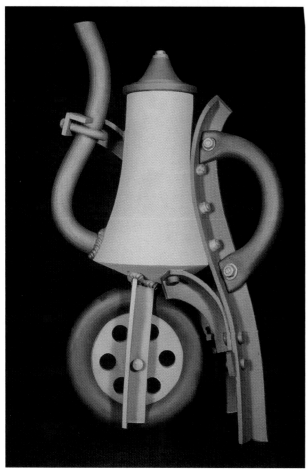

"It was through my wish to emulate the quartz and an exploration of various methods of clay construction on a large scale that I discovered the extruder. My discovery of the extruder has proven to be a catalyst also in the exploration of the vessel form."

Richard Montgomery

Jake Jacobson, Mono Teapot, 16" x 11" x 8", 1987, thrown and extruded white ware clay, then assembled. "This piece was covered with a base coat of terra sigillata and fired to cone 05. The iridescent metallic colors were developed by layering and multiple firing of liquid lusters. As many as 18 firings in the cone 020 range were required to produce the final color." Photo by Jean Jacobson.

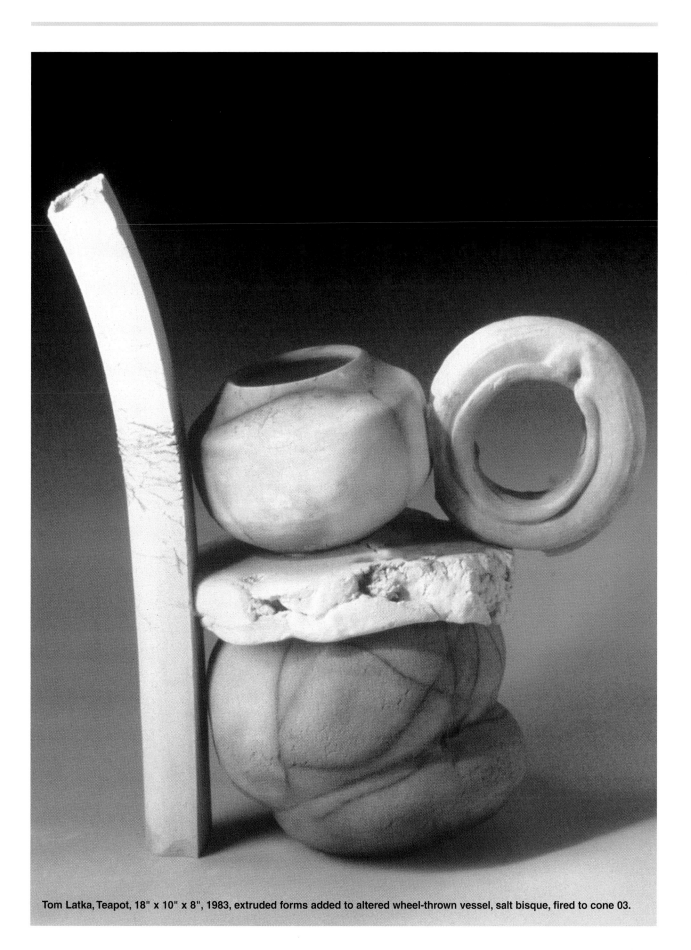

Tom Latka, Teapot, 18" x 10" x 8", 1983, extruded forms added to altered wheel-thrown vessel, salt bisque, fired to cone 03.

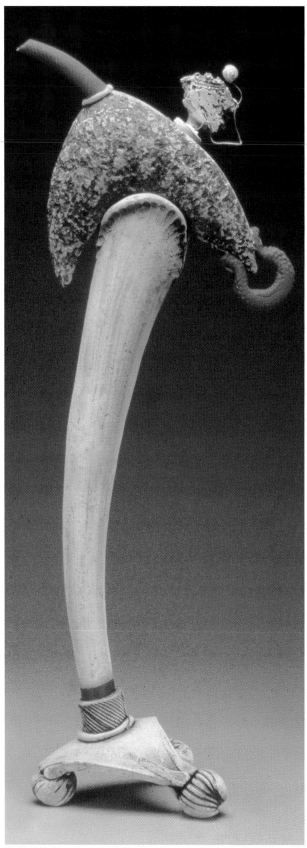

Kathy Triplett, Teapot, 29" x 6" x 6", 1998, hand-built and extruded earthenware clay, fired to cone 05. Photo by Tim Barnwell.

extruder, use a pottery cut-off wire. This is a thin piece of wire with two small dowel handles attached to each end.

♦ Spiral wire. To make a decorative effect when cutting through a block of clay.

♦ Common cheese cutters are handy to remove a quantity of clay quickly and easily. Remove the plastic roller on the cutter so you can cut as deeply as needed.

♦ Ware boards to stack extruded forms. We use pieces of wood approximately 12" x 36". Ware boards enable you to move a group of items around the studio easily, rather than having to move each piece individually.

♦ Canvas. Cover your work surface with a piece of canvas cut approximately 18" x 24" to keep the clay from sticking.

♦ Fettling knife to cut and trim extruded forms into the desired shapes.

♦ Rolling pins to smooth out slabs when they are placed on the canvas sheets or over molds. We use a large rolling pin because its weight makes the job easier.

♦ Templates. When cutting a form to a specific shape we sometimes use a template made from ⅛" Masonite. Heavy paper, Styrofoam, and cardboard also work.

♦ Sponges. Smooth rough edges of clay and apply small amounts of water when needed, such as when joining two pieces of clay.

♦ Banding wheel. These small, portable turntables allow you to turn the object you are working on rather than having to walk around the object.

♦ A rib to compact and shape the clay. Ribs are made from rubber, wood, metal, or traditionally, bone. We use a metal serrated rib with one flat side and small teeth indentations on the other. The serrated edge scores the join between two pieces of clay.

♦ Plastic sheets or drop cloths to control the rate of drying in the clay and extruded forms.

♦ Five gallon buckets to store water and to mix glazes in.

♦ Rubber gloves to protect you from absorbing chemicals through your pores. They also keep your hands dry so your fingers and nails don't crack so easily.

♦ An OSHA certified respirator to reduce the inhalation of dust and other chemicals that must be worn whenever working with dry powders.

♦ Mixer or electric drill to expedite glaze blending. When the glaze is the consistency you desire, strain the glaze though a nylon paint sieve that fits a five gallon bucket.

♦ A paint spray gun to apply glazes. Wear your respirator.

Michael Sherrill, Teapot, 18" x 18" x 6", low-fired earthenware extrusions altered and assembled, fired to cone 03. Photo by Tim Barnwell.

♦ A kiln to fire extruded forms. We have a variety of kilns, including a high-fired gas kiln, a salt bisque kiln, and two electric kilns. We recently upgraded our electric kilns, purchasing kilns with a computer to monitor the firing speed and temperature. It's like having grown children.

Tips to Help You Get Started

♦ If you have never used an extruder before, familiarize yourself with the machine. Note where the feed mouth and the chamber are located and, if using a manual extruder, how the plunger operates. Try attaching and removing the die a few times- it's easier to learn this step before the clay is added.

♦ If you are using an extruder that can be operated both vertically and horizontally, use the extruder in the vertical position first. This will acquaint you with the operation of the extruder and enable you to get a "feel" for the machine.

♦ Start small. Extrude small sections of clay when first starting so you can understand how the extruder works. You will also learn if the clay you are using is the right consistency. After you feel comfortable with small forms, graduate to larger ones, altering the clay consistency as need be.

♦ Always check the size of your kiln and the kiln shelves and create pieces that will fit on them. This seems an obvious point but when we started out, we became so focused on the extrusions that we sometimes forgot the size limitations and constructed pieces too large to fire in our kiln.

♦ Prepare a work area. Extrusions can exit the

Madeline Kaczmarczyk, Teapots Waiting for the Flood, 12" x 8" x 6", 1998, thrown forms with extruded appendages, fired to cone 03. Photo by the artist.

machine rapidly and you will need a place to set them. Have sheets of canvas cloth readily available so you can place the extrusions directly on them. Keep the canvas free from clay scraps, as they will stick to the canvas and become embedded in the extruded clay.

♦ Have your tools readily available. When working specifically with a large cylinder die to construct slabs, it is helpful to have the fettling knife and cut off wire nearby to cut the cylinder open before laying it down on the canvas.

♦ Have plenty of clay available. Extrusions works well with stoneware, earthenware, or porcelain. Extruders can work as quickly as clay can be fed into them and if you plan to work in a series (pro-

duce a quantity of one form), having a supply of clay ready will eliminate the need to stop and gather more clay, breaking the continuity and flow of the extrusions.

♦ Before starting to work, remove any pieces of clay that have hardened on the mouth of the extruder. This will keep any hard pieces from getting into your extruded forms.

♦ Be patient and don't forget to play. More than likely, you won't know what to do with the first extrusions. Make a stack of them and then start playing with them by slicing, twisting, rolling, or pulling them into various shapes and configurations. Use them at different stages of hardness. It is through these experiments that new ideas are formed.

James Dunaway, Teapot, 10" x 16", 1993, grouping of extrusions, combined and altered, fired to cone 10. Photo by the artist.

Chapter 6
Putting It to Use - Extruder Projects

The projects in this chapter illustrate just a few of the creative and functional uses for the extruder. The extruder is a tool, just like a potter's wheel or a slab roller. Because extrusions are machine generated and pushed through a static die, they can produce endless quantities of identical forms. This is a desirable feature in industries that utilize the extruder for mass production, but the extruder can also assist in formulating creative impulses and concepts. Once you begin to understand the three-dimensional qualities that the extruder is capable of producing, the manipulation of the clay becomes a personal statement.

Learning to appreciate the subtleties and nuances of how, as a tool, the extruder can enhance your work is a process. Jim Bailey, of Bailey Ceramic Supply, likens learning the extruder to that of a musical instrument. When a pianist takes up the guitar, quite often they don't "get it" because the instruments are so different. It takes a certain amount of diligence and study to master and bring dimension to a new instrument. So it is with the extruder when compared to the potter's wheel. They are so different that time is a crucial element in learning to use the tool as a vehicle for the creative voice.

When working with any new tool, there is a learning curve required to fully grasp the concepts and idiosyncrasies of that tool, and the extruder is no exception. Certain requirements will become evident, like lining the die up correctly, the best consistency of the clay, the strength and shape of the die required to extrude the desired form. If you stick with it, you will resolve any problems and in the process gain a better understanding of the interaction between the extruder and the clay.

The extrusions themselves will sometimes trigger new solutions for old problems. For example, if handles have been a challenge or a process you want to expedite, follow the steps in the handle project (page 60). This will enable you to make your own but will also demonstrate the ease of the process. You can then modify our idea and construct a die that suits your needs and personal design tastes.

Many of the projects demonstrate the versatility of a particular die. Often the simplicity of one extruded form can be expanded to include other forms using the same die. We are able to extrude wine coolers, umbrella stands, and planters all from the same die simply by shortening or lengthening

Jean Latka. The extruded handle is made using a solid die and can take any design or configuration the imagination dreams up. Handles can be elaborate, with dips and ridges, or simple flat surfaces to manipulate or decorate at a later time.

the extrusion.

Deciding how to finish the extruded pieces can lead you into a whole new realm of the ceramic arts. Surface treatment is as varied as the flowers on a mountaintop. Glazing, which is the glass surface that sits on a vessel once it has been fired, can be done in numerous ways to achieve different effects. Glazes can be glossy, matte, dry, or satiny. Slips applied over or under a glaze can yield a variety of characteristics and if these are combined with colorants, a palette of color as wide as the rainbow can be achieved. If the piece is functional, to be used for eating or drinking, use a glaze that is smooth when fired, is nontoxic, and washed easily. Sculptural forms allow for more variety in the finished surface because they are experienced with the eye and hand so the glaze or slip application can be as organic as the artist prefers. The projects that follow demonstrate the steps taken to make a particular object. How you choose to finish them will allow you to experiment with the numerous options that are possible in the world of glazing.

These projects are meant to instruct and inspire and to exhibit the various methods that an extruder can encompass. Once the variety has been established, your own ideas will flow like the clay from your extruder.

Richard Montgomery, Vase, 9" x 5½" x 5", 1991, extrusions connected and altered, fired to cone 03. Photo by the artist.

Jean Latka, Dish with Extruded Handles, 18" x 9" x 3", 1998, extruded slab cut open to make a slab, press molded into plaster mold with extrusions from the handle die applied on the rim, fired to cone 10 reduction.

Jean Latka, Bowl, 14" x 3" x 4", 1998, group of extrusions using the handle die, draped into a plaster mold, fired to cone 10 reduction.

Attaching a two finger handle to the mug.

Solid Die Projects

Can You Handle This?

The handle is the most common form associated with the extruder. It was through this straightforward method of mass production that potters came to understand the concept of extrusion and see the labor and time saving benefits. However, most potters find the look of the straight extruded handle too mechanical. Probably the number one criticism of extrusions is that they are rigid and sterile looking. It is possible, though, to create a pleasing handle. Remember that extrusions are the starting point, not the end step in the process, and further manipulation of the clay will yield a softer, more complementary attachment. Extrusions are versatile. They can be used exactly how they exit the machine or they can be worked, creating the look you desire. Simply pulling the base of the extrusion to a taper is an immediate way to give the handle a more harmonious look.

We utilize a round, one-fingered handle for our mugs and attach a thumb-stop when the handle is leather-hard. This style is comfortable, balances well in the hand, and looks good on the mug. Using the same die, it is also possible to make an oval form from the extruded strap for a two-fingered mug. Both handles are simple to make.

1. Throw a mug.

2. Extrude a handle 3" long and shape it into a circle that is about 1½" in diameter.

3. Using a fork or serrated metal rib, score the area and add slip to the area on the mug where the handle will be placed.

4. Attach the handle to the mug by pressing it firmly to the scored area. Let dry until leather-hard.

The die we used to make the mug handle. We made this die, but there are a multitude of handle dies commercially available. If you want to make your own, refer to page 40 for instructions.

We pulled the base of this extrusion to alter its shape.

The handle extrusions.

Shaping the thumb-stop.

The thumb-stop in place on the handle.

5. Score and add slip to attach a small ball of clay to the top of the handle. This small ball of clay will be the thumb-stop, the resting place for the thumb that provides balance to the fingers while the mug is in use.

6. Smooth any rough edges, fire to bisque, and finish as desired.

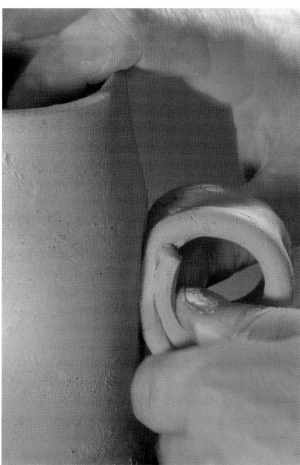

Attaching the circular handle to the mug.

Jean Latka, Pitcher, 14" x 6" x 6", 1999, extrusion from cylinder die, altered and thrown on potter's wheel, fired to cone 10 reduction.

The finished plate.

The hump mold plate before firing.

The four extrusions laid around the hump mold.

The solid die we used to make the lip for a plate. You can make your own die (see page 40) or buy one.

The extruded straps.

Hump Mold Plate

A variation of the handle die is used to make lips for dinner plates and platters. This is a simple method to accent the rims of pieces, creating a dramatic statement.

1. Extrude four handle straps about 2" longer than the length of the hump mold.

2. Lay the straps around the hump mold, overlapping the ends.

3. With a fork, score the edges of the extruded straps where the straps and the plate meet.

4. With a fettling knife, cut a square or rectangle from a clay slab. This should be large enough to completely cover the hump mold and the handles.

5. Lay the clay square or rectangle over the convex side of the hump mold, on top of the extruded straps.

6. Apply pressure to securely join the straps to the slab.

7. When the plate is leather-hard, trim off any excess clay.

8. Turn the plate over on a flat work surface. Press down in the middle to flatten.

9. Smooth any rough edges, fire to bisque, and finish as desired.

Cutting the slab to size.

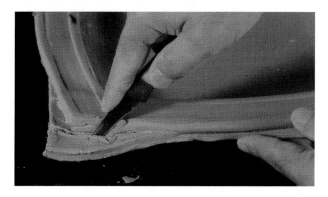

To add a textural dimension, attach extrusions directly onto the convex side of a molded platter.

The solid we die used to make the extrusions for the textural rim around the wall platter. You can make your own die (see page 40) or buy one.

The extruded straps.

Wall Platter

A readily available and inexpensive mold for a platter is a child's sledding dish. Large and perfectly round, these can be purchased from any toy store. Before laying on the clay, cover the sledding dish with polyester or any fabric that will stretch and not wrinkle.

1. Extrude 30 handle straps that are each 18" long.

2. Place a round slab or thrown plate in the middle of the mold. Score the edge where the rim straps will be attached.

3. Cut the straps into 6" lengths and attach them in an arch shape, one end on top of the other, working in an outward, circular direction to the edge of the plate. Place the ends of the arches on top of each other and completely encircle the plate. Then place another row of arches in the blank areas.

4. To complete the platter, create a lip by extruding an 18" long flat strap from the handle die. You'll need to change dies. Place this lip along the edge of the final row of curved extrusions. Press down firmly to bond the two together.

5. Place a small pillow on the top of the platter, followed by a throwing bat. With one hand under the mold and the other on top of the bat, flip the platter over. Flatten as necessary to make it stable.

6. Smooth any rough edges, fire to bisque, and finish as desired.

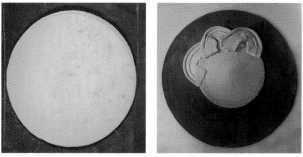

A round slab.

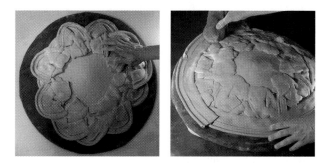

The fired bowl.

The solid die we used. You can make your own die (see page 40) or buy one.

The extruded handle straps.

The unfired bowl.

"Big-Eared" Bowl

This "Big Eared" Bowl came upon the scene in the 1980s and was an immediate success. The traditional bowl form is made whimsical and sculptural with the addition of over-sized extruded handles, creating the impression that "Big Ears" is a presence that needs to be heard.

1. Using three pounds of pugged clay, throw an upright bowl with a vigorous, well defined lip on the potter's wheel.

2. While the pot is still fresh from throwing, alter the lip by simultaneously pinching and pounding the clay as shown.

3. Squeeze the bowl into an oval shape.

4. Extrude two handle straps, each about 8" in length.

5. When the altered bowl has stiffened, score the lip in the areas that were pinched.

6. Fold the extrusions and pinch them at the bottom of the fold to form handles.

7. Place the handles on the scored slipped areas of the bowl, pressing deliberately to secure them to the bowl.

8. When the bowl has dried to the leather-hard stage, flip it over onto a pillow or piece of foam

and remove the excess clay from the bottom using a cheese slicer.

9. Smooth any rough edges, fire to bisque, and finish as desired.

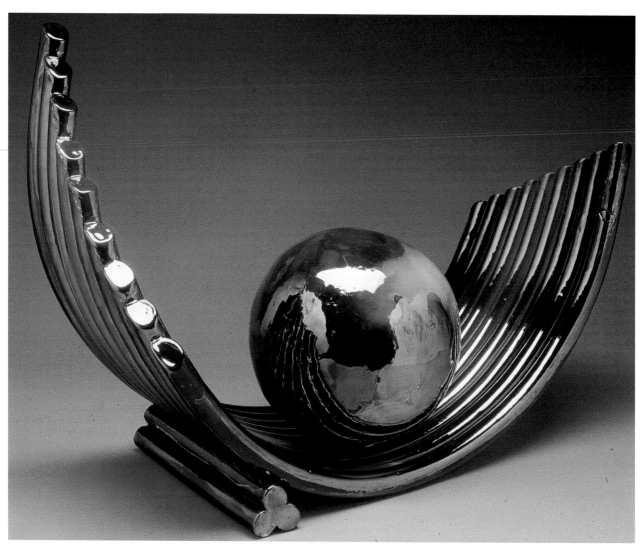

Jutta Golas, Wave and Sphere, 16" x 18" x 8", 1999, extruded forms laid into a mold, low-fire lusters, fired to cone 012. Photo by the artist.

Coils

The coil is a very basic form created using a solid die. Called ropes, snakes, and worms, these lengths of clay are often a child's introduction to the ceramic world. Even though they are simplistic, coils provide the fundamental source for some of the most unusual and intricate vessels created.

The coil dates back to 7000 B.C., when ceramics was still in its infancy. An imprint of a basket made of coils was found in an archeological excavation of a clay floor. This technique, which was in use thousands of years before the introduction of the potter's wheel, has been employed throughout the history of ceramics. Coil built objects have been discovered throughout the world, from China to Africa and the Americas. The famous monumental wine urns of Cyprus, commonly referred to as "honeymoon" pots because they could hold two people, were built from coils, as were the giant horse sculptures of Southern India. Coils are the traditional form of construction for the American Indian and are

Gene Koss, Bundle Stack Series, 3' x 10', 1975, extruded coils stacked and assembled, fired to cone 5. Photo by the artist.

still actively used to build their handsome, pit-fired vessels.

Where consistency of shape is a priority, coils must be carefully made. In English potteries, coils were placed between wooden guides and rolled out using rolling pins to insure uniform thickness. Each coil was meticulously attached and joined at the ends to prevent the pot from developing any irregularities.

To hasten the drying process so pots can be made more quickly, many potters work on two or three coiled vessels at a time. Korean potters, known to make jars 3' to 4' feet high, use a small oil lamp suspended inside the pot with a string to hasten the stiffening of the pot so that the coiling can proceed more rapidly.

There is a paradox to this simple technique. It is at once easy to understand yet complex enough that a master crafts-man can produce objects of beauty only after years of patient study.

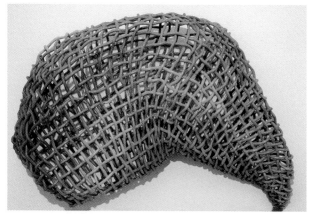

Phyllis Kudder-Sullivan, Pod 53, 19" x 27" x 9", 1995, woven sculpture made from extruded coils, fired to cone 03. Photo by Joseph Sullivan.

A finished Recoil Vessel.

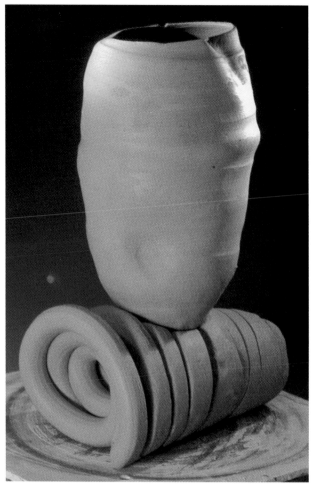

An unfired variation of the Recoil Vessel.

The die we used to make 1" coils.

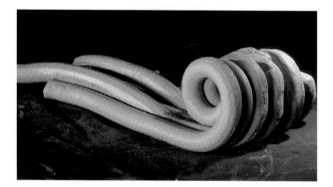

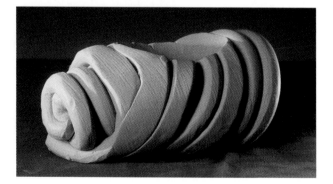

Recoil Vessel

1. Construct the coil foot by extruding seven 1" coils, 18" long.

2. Lay six of the coils together, with some stacked, some curved, and some straight. To create a more interesting bas, don't line up the coils in straight rows.

3. Starting at one end, roll the grouped coils, rolling one side more tightly than the other. This will create a seashell-like form.

4. Using a round object, such as a baseball, make an indentation on top of the rolled coils. This is where the body of the vessel will eventually rest. Set aside.

5. Using seven pounds of pugged clay, throw the vessel form on the potter's wheel. Thin the top 4" of the vessel as much as possible.

6. Press your dry hands together along the lip of the vessel and pull up, tearing the clay as you move along. Continue until the entire lip has been torn.

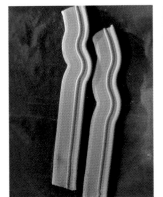

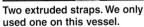

The die we used for the handle strap.

Two extruded straps. We only used one on this vessel.

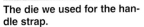

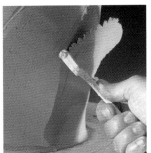

7. Alter the form of the vessel by pushing the sides into an oval shape.

8. Score and slip the inside of the torn lip on the vessel.

9. Extrude a handle strap about 18" long.

10. Score and slip one side of the strap and place it lightly on the inside of your arm, scored side up.

11. Starting with the end closest to your fingers, place the strap on the inside of the vessel, using the other hand to press down firmly to attach it to the vessel. Let dry to leather-hard.

12. With the vessel upright, use a cheese slicer tool to remove excess clay, sculpting the base to fit the indentation on the coiled foot.

13. Smooth any rough edges and allow the two pieces to dry. Fire each piece separately.

14. Glue the pieces together, using a commercial adhesive such as silicon or PL 400.

15. Finish as desired.

Richard Meyer, Architectural Jar, 14" x 8" x 8", 1989, thrown form with extruded elements on lid, fired in raku kiln to cone 010. Photo by the artist.

Mike Ruybal, Jar with an Attitude, 24" x 12" x 6", 1973, extruded base with extruded lid attached, fired to cone 03. Photo by the artist.

Hollow Die Projects

Hollow extrusions are more complicated to make and extrude but they are worth the extra effort because they create a more interesting extrusion. The hollow die pushes the extruded form into a more sculptural realm, providing more variety and the options for greater artistic expression.

The tree-shaped die we used. Any hollow die with a 1" opening will work for napkin rings.

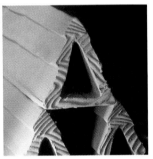

The extrusion.

Christmas Tree Napkin Rings

We made a die in the shape of Christmas tree, which has proven to be adaptable to a variety of uses. Letting it flow from the extruder and compressing the base, it makes a beautiful vase; cut into small 2" sections, it is a handy, uniform size for napkin holders, glaze tests, and handles on mugs.

1. Make a 14" extrusion.

2. Just before the leather-hard stage, slice the extrusion into 1" sections with a fettling knife.

3. Let dry and smooth off all the sharp edges. Finish as desired.

The Christmas tree die is ideal for glaze tests. These extruded forms stand vertically in the kiln and have a large base upon which to write pertinent test information. It is important that glaze tests be applied to a vertical surface to provide a true result of what the glaze will do at a variety of temperatures. Will it run off? Does it crawl? The more information you can acquire from a test, the more assurance you have to mix up large quantities of the glaze. After firing, the tests can be strung together with wire or rope for easy reference and storage.

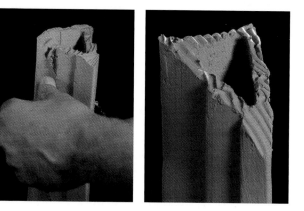

Smashed Vase

Vases are our favorite thing to make with the hollow Christmas die. The finished vases can encompass everything from the straightforward extrusion to the whimsical form. The bottom of this vase exits the machine first. It's important to form a mass at the bottom because the vase is top heavy.

1. Make a 4" or 5" clay extrusion but don't remove the extrusion from the machine.

2. Stop the extruder and pinch the bottom together.

3. Paddle the base flat.

4. Use a needle tool to poke a hole in the extrusion. This is a necessary to keep the form from imploding, or collapsing in on itself. This happens if a vacuum is created by sealing off the bottom.

5. Start extruding again. When the extrusion is about 16" long, gently pull on the form to remove it from the extruder and set it upright on the worktable.

6. To form the lip of the vase, we used a spiral wire made from a spring pulled taut. Let the vase dry to the point where you can pull the wire through the top of the form without distorting the vase.

7. Smooth any rough edges, fire to bisque, and finish as desired.

Nick and Tom Latka, Extruder Fountain at the Terry Riley Building, Pueblo, Colorado, 6' x 6' x 2'6", 1985, Nick Latka pictured, extruded tubes and fountain border, fired to cone 10.

John Toki and assistant Bryan Vansell working on a large extruded sculpture, 1989. Photo by Diane Pantone.

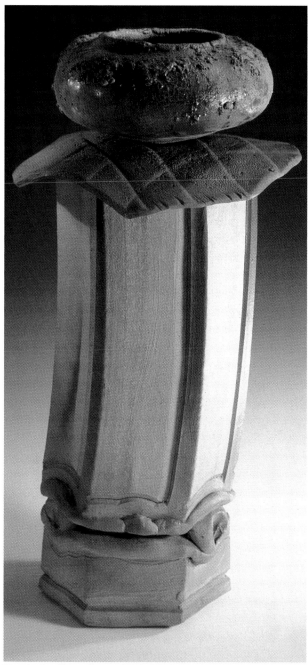

Tom Latka, Up or Down, Works Both Ways, 30" x 9" x 10", 1987, extruded vessel with wheel-thrown vase as lid, fired to cone 10.

Tom Latka, Vase with Vase on Top, 18" x 6" x 6", 2000, extruded base from a hollow die and wheel-thrown vase as lid, fired to cone 6.

Cylinders

Of all the dies we use in our studio the cylinder die has proven to be the most versatile simply because we utilize the extruded cylinder form to make everything from two-dimensional tiles and wall pieces to three-dimensional sconce lighting fixtures and sculptural forms.

A round hollow die is used to extrude cylinders and there are many of these dies commercially available. If you wish to construct your own, you will need the help of a machinist. The die must be made of metal because of the extreme pressure exerted on it.

A little smaller cylinder works well for a flower pot.

Smaller yet makes a perfect wine cooler.

The cylinder form large enough to make an umbrella stand.

Unfired cylindrical forms made with a round hollow die.

Umbrella Stands, Wine Coolers, and Planters

This project requires a round 8" hollow die and an expansion box. The only difference between the wine cooler, umbrella stand, and planter is height. The umbrella stand is the tallest, at about 20". It must be tall enough to hold umbrellas and heavy enough so it won't fall over.

1. Extrude a 20" long cylinder. With dry hands, gently remove it from the extruder.

2. The clay coming out of the extruder will be uneven and unless it is straightened out, the cylinder will not set level on the table when it is removed from the extruder. To straighten the bottom of the extrusion, use a fettling knife to cut around the cylinder while it is still hanging from the machine.

3. When the desired length has been extruded, gently pull the clay from the extruder. This step requires dry hands to create friction between the clay and your hands but it also requires a gentle touch so as not to distort the extrusion too much. Quickly set the extruded cylinder on a piece of canvas.

The round hollow die we used.

The expansion box mounted on the extruder.

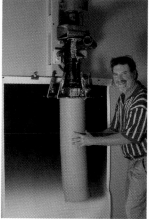

Tom Latka with an extrusion.

4. Extrusions of this size will have a tendency to lean to one side. Let the form set until just before the leather-hard stage. Use a carpenter's square to mark the top and cut it so it's even.

5. Invert the form onto a potter's wheel. While the wheel is turning, use a needle tool to cut a straight edge around the top of the form. Remove the cylinder from the potter's wheel.

6. Throw a flat plate, ⅜" thick by 9" in diameter, on the potter's wheel.

7. Score and slip the bottom edge of the cylinder and the flange of the thrown plate. Center the cylinder on the plate.

8. Press the outside edge of the flat thrown plate onto the cylinder.

9. Score and slip the top of the cylinder. Using the coil plus die, extrude a coil 20" long and secure it to the top of the cylinder.

10. Throw a vigorous lip. We have always thought that a pot, like a sentence, requires punctuation. The capital letter is to a sentence what a lip is to a pot. The foot is the period.

11. If desired, add handles (refer to page 63 for instructions for handles).

12. Smooth any rough edges, fire to bisque, and finish as desired.

Garth Edwards and Raymond Serrano, Entry Tiles at the Seattle Children's Theatre, 1993, extruded slabs made into tiles and carved, fired to cone 6. Photo by the artist.

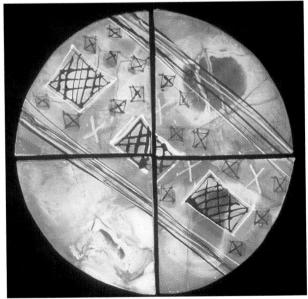

M. Aktal, Wall Mandala, 30" diameter, 2000, cut and altered extruded slabs, fired to cone 03 with acrylic over paint. Photo by the artist.

Slabs

In the ceramic world, a slab is a flat sheet of clay. Slabs can vary in thickness from paper thin to several inches thick, depending on the size of a project. Slabs are exciting and versatile forms to extrude because they are the building block for many different forms.

Slabs ½" thick work best for the forms we create. This thickness keeps cracking and warping at a minimum yet is thick enough to manipulate comfortably. These sheets of clay can be draped, slumped, and carved or used to construct murals and make tiles. Slabs can be cut up and the individual pieces applied as decorative accents or they can remain untouched, glazed, and fired to be incorporated in wall pieces.

The advantage of using a pugmill to construct slabs instead of a slab roller or rolling pin is that the pugmill compresses the clay as it is forced through the die. Under compression, the matrix of the clay particles are forced together,

strengthening their bond. With a slab roller or rolling pin, the opposite happens. Clay becomes compressed in the middle of the slab and stretched around the edges. When the clay particles are stretched, the bond and structural integrity between the particles weakens. This allows more cracking and warping in the finished piece.

Clay has a memory. However it is worked - thrown on the potter's wheel, pugged, rolled, or extruded - the clay particles want to stay in the configuration of their original composition. When extruding a cylinder, the particles become aligned in a circular pattern and when the cylinder is cut open and laid flat, the particles are still in a cylindrical pattern so there is the tendency for the slab to curl up along the cut edge. Working with the memory can at times be beneficial but when using a cylinder for a slab, you'll need to compensate for its desire to curl. Fortunately, it's as simple as flipping the slab over so that when the slab curls it meets the resistance of the table or any other flat form and will remain a flat sheet of clay.

Tom Latka, Could Be a Memorial, 3' x 20" x 14", 1988, extruded slabs pressed into plaster mold, extruded top using the "D" die.

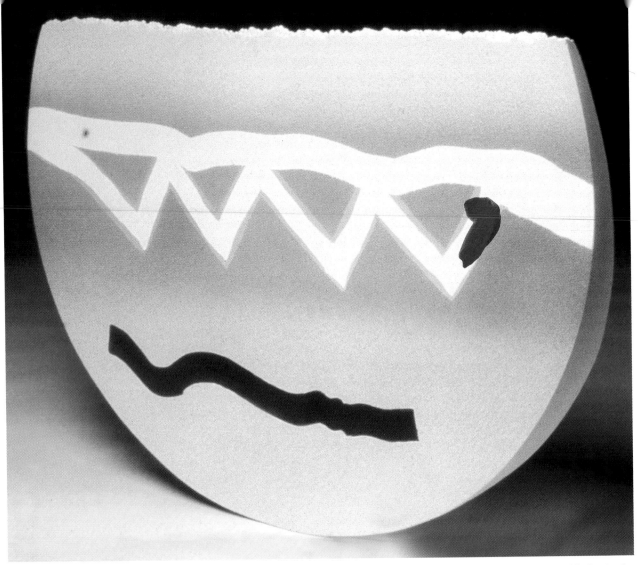

Nick Latka, Sail Away, 20" x 14" x 6", 1984, assembled extruded slabs, airbrush design, fired to cone 03. Photo by the artist.

Making a Slab from an Extruded Cylinder

1. Extrude a cylinder and remove it from the machine.

2. Place the cylinder on a table and use a fettling knife or needle tool to slice up the length of the cylinder.

3. Working quickly, open the cut cylinder. At this point the cylinder becomes extremely unstable because the geometry of the form has been breached. Gingerly lay the clay on a piece of canvas.

4. The top and bottom edges of the slab are ragged because the cylinder was pulled from the extrud-

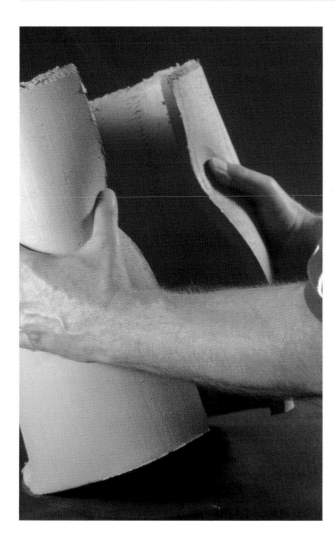

Extruded slabs, stacked and ready.

er and the slab itself will be wavy. Place a piece of canvas over the slab and flatten it with a rolling pin.

5. Cut off the ragged edges with a fettling knife.

6. Invert the slab by gripping the two pieces of canvas at the edges and flipping it over. The two pieces of canvas are bonded to the clay so it will be easy to turn the slab over without dropping the clay. Flipping the slab will allow it to dry perfectly flat.

7. If making a number of slabs, stack them with canvas between each clay slab.

The unfired, assembled wall piece.

The finished wall piece.

Handle extrusions to use as decorative elements.

Wall Diptych

We draped our slabs over a junkyard glass TV screen to get a shallow bowl form, but you can use a flat slab or use any slightly curved surface as a mold.

1. Construct a slab large enough to cut a 10" x 14" rectangle. (See page 85 for instructions on making a slab from a cylindrical extrusion.) Lay the slab on a piece of canvas.

2. Using material of your choice, make a 10" x 14" template. Place the template on the slab and cut around it with a fettling knife.

3. Gripping the edges of the canvas, lift the slab and flip it onto the curved mold (in our case, the TV screen).

4. To apply the foot to the plate, center the TV screen or mold on the potter's wheel.

5. Score and slip the area where the foot will be applied.

6. Using the coil die, extrude a coil about 18" long and lay it over the scored and slipped area. Apply pressure to adhere the foot to the slab.

7. Throw the foot on the slab, bringing it up to a height of about 1". Bevel the foot inward to allow the option of hanging the finished piece on the wall.

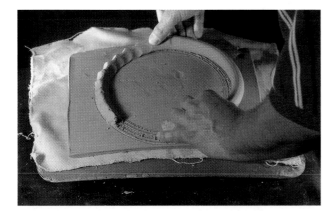

8. When the dish has dried to the leather-hard stage, remove it from the mold, take off the canvas, and set it on a table. Make any adjustments to ensure that it is level.

9. Score and add slip to the area where the decorative extrusions will be applied.

10. Use a handle die to extrude 16" of clay to use as decorative elements.

11. Pull a spiral wire through a block of clay 2" thick, 2" wide, and 6" long to create a decorative effect.

12. Score and slip the are and attach the decorative handle extrusion and the wire cut piece of clay to the slab, pressing down firmly to secure. Don't press so hard that you distort the composition.

13. Use a coil die to extrude 12 coils 1" in diameter.

14. Score and slip and add these to the slab.

15. Smooth any rough edges, fire to bisque, and finish as desired.

16. Create a similar composition on another slab to complete an interesting diptych wall piece.

Joe May of the Pueblo Community College presenting Jean's platter to President Clinton.

Jean Latka with the President's Platter.

The President's Platter

Small hollow extrusions are a great way to create accents for larger pieces. We often use a die we designed and call the "D" die because its shape resembles the letter D. The extrusions made with this die can be manipulated in a variety of ways to make interesting shapes for decorative additions.

Jean created this platter as a gift for President Clinton when he visited the Pueblo Community College in our hometown. She decided to create a piece with an exaggerated extruded border with bright majolica stains floating in an abstract pattern. The platter measures 18" in diameter and is 2" thick.

1. Using ten pounds of freshly pugged clay, throw a platter about 18" in diameter on the potter's wheel. Leave an extra amount of clay on the lip of the platter for added support for the extruded lip that will be added later.

2. When the platter has dried to the leather-hard stage, score the top of the lip using a fork and apply slip.

On the left is the extrusion made with the D die and on the right is the hollow coil.

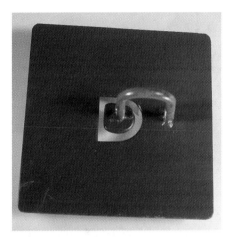

The D die Jean used to make the lip for the platter.

3. Use the hollow coil D die to extrude a lip 18" long. Take special care to support the extrusion as it exits the machine to prevent any tears or breaks.

4. Lay the extrusions on a ware board and wet them lightly with a damp sponge. Carefully lift the round hollow extrusions and gently place them around the lip of the platter. Once they are in place, carefully apply enough pressure to bond the extrusions to the platter.

5. To cover where the ends of the lip pieces meet, construct a decorated juncture. This can be done using the "D" die. Extrude a piece approximately 12" long and flatten it with the edge side of the extrusion up. Cut this into 3" pieces. Score and slip the juncture and apply the flattened extruded pieces. Apply pressure to adhere, being careful not to smudge or mangle the extrusions. Let dry until leather-hard.

6. Invert the platter onto a soft pillow and use a cheese cutter to trim the excess clay from the bottom of the platter.

7. Turn the platter over and lightly press down to flatten the bottom.

8. Smooth any rough edges, fire to bisque, and finish as desired.

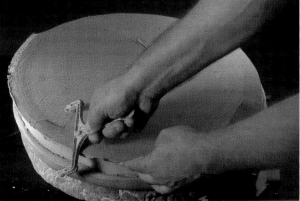

The unfired woven tile.

The finished piece.

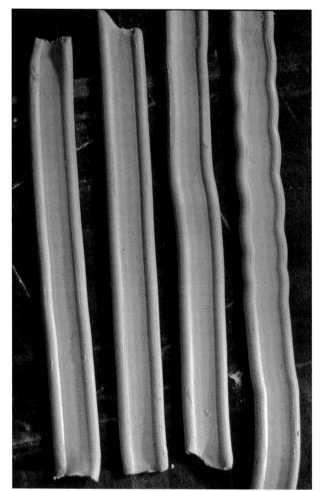

The extrusions made with the handle die.

Woven Tile

Tiles are a delightful way to add texture, dimension, and color to a room. This small, three-dimensional piece isn't intended for functional use, but as an architectural statement and works well in a variety of design settings.

1. Using the handle die, extrude four handle straps that are about 6" in length.

2. Use a wood template and cut out a 4" square from a slab of clay (see page 82 for instructions to make a slab).

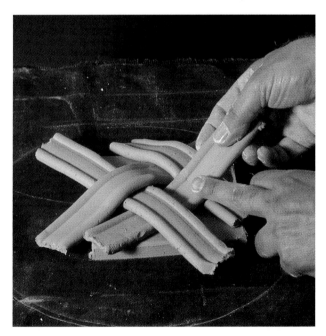

3. Score and slip the back of the handle extrusions and the corners of the square tile. Attach one of the extrusions to the tile.

4. Continue to add the handle extrusions, weaving the straps between each other.

5. Trim off excess clay.

6. Smooth any rough edges, fire to bisque, and finish as desired.

The unfired ribbed tile

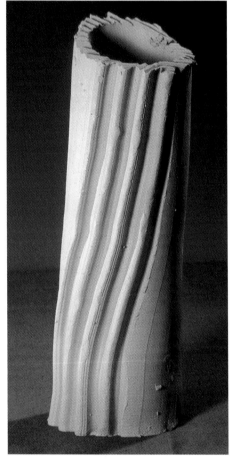

The extrusion made with the ribbed die.

The ribbed cylinder die we used.

The finished piece.

Ribbed Tile

The ribbed tile adds the element of bold lines to the design of the tile and provides an area where interesting glazing techniques can be used. When installed, they can be arranged in a herringbone pattern or woven to create a basket pattern on a wall.

1. Extrude a cylinder 8" long using the ribbed cylinder die.

2. Slice the cylinder lengthwise, open it, and lay it flat on a piece of canvas.

3. It is possible to position the template in different ways on the slab, creating tiles with an assortment of patterns. Position a 6" square wood template as desired and cut it out.

4. Smooth any rough edges, fire to bisque, and finish as desired.

Tom Latka, The Vase Dance, 16" x 5" x 3", 1982, hollow extruded form split down the sides, fired to cone 01. Photo by the artist.

Jim Robison. Vase, 24" x 12" x 8", 2000, extruded strips laid on slip-decorated and scored slabs, fired to cone 8 in reduction. Photo by the artist.

Clay Daggett, Tall Sculpture, 7' x 12", 1994, altered industrial extrusions, fired cone 6 oxidation. Photo by the artist.

Alessio Tasca, Cosmagnon, 4' x 18" x 18", 1978, industrial extrusions, carved and fired to cone 8 reduction. Photo by the artist.

Tom and Jean Latka, Intersection Mural, 8' x 12' x 6", 1997, altered and manipulated extruded forms, fired to cone 03.

Detail of Intersection Mural.

Jack Sures installing a mural at the Canadian Museum of Civilization in 1989. Photo by Don Hall.

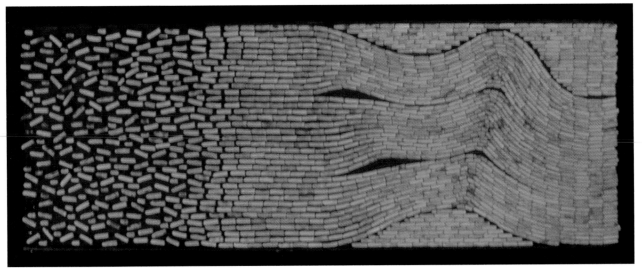

Jack Sures, Firelight Mural, 12' x 8' x 3", 1989, installation mural exhibited at the Grand Priz in Mino, Japan, earthenware extrusions with engobes added, fired to cone 03. Photo by Don Hall.

Jean Latka, Log Jam, 14' x 12', 1995, mosaic mural using tiles from extruded slabs, earthenware with majolica glaze and Mason stains, fired to cone 01.

Detail of Log Jam.

Ken Williams, 6th Avenue Plaza Carved Arch, 12' x 7' x 7', 1992, extruded bricks stacked and carved, fired to cone 10. Photo by the artist.

Robert Harrison, Tile –X, 25' x 25' x 22', 1985, sculpture constructed from drain tile from the Western Clay Manufacturing Co. in Helena, Mont., site of the Archie Bray Foundation, fired to cone 6. Photo by the artist.

Roberta Griffith, Nezu Reflections, 7' x 11' x 63", 1998, fired to cone 06. Photo by the artist.

Nicholas Wood, Houses in Motion- Lineage I, 70" x 70" x 5½", 1983, terracotta clay extruded and altered, fired to cone 03. "I use a manual extruder with aluminum dies to achieve the size and length of extrusions, then I lightly hand roll and compress them to soften or decrease and increase their final thickness." Photo by the artist.

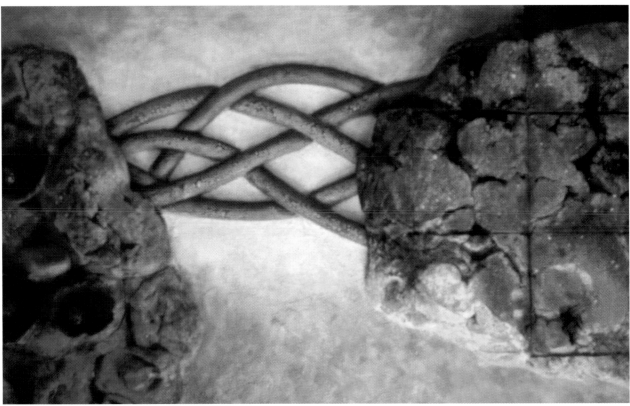

Tom Latka, Synapsis, 8' x 4', 1996, large masses of clay joined by weaving extruded coils, fired to cone 01 oxidation.

Detail of Kiln God, showing method of construction. Photo by the artist.

David Porter, Kiln God, 12' x 8' x 6', 1989, extruded coils meshed together and used as armature, then sculpted, fired to cone 6. Photo by the artist.

Tom Latka, Flameboy, 12' diameter, 1992, large mural made from sculpted, altered, and press molded extruded elements, fired to cone 5.

Jack Sures, detail of Air, Earth, Water, Fire, 12' x 20' x 2", 1990, mural with earthenware extrusions on curved wall at the Museum of Civilization Hall in Ottawa, Ontario, Canada, fired to cone 04. Photo by the artist.

Alessio Tasca, Colroigo, 3' x 3' x 3', 1986, industrial extrusion, carved and fired to cone 8 reduction. Photo by the artist.

Jerry Rothman, Figure A, 10' x 6' x 10', industrial extrusions cut in block sections and stacked, fired to cone 6.

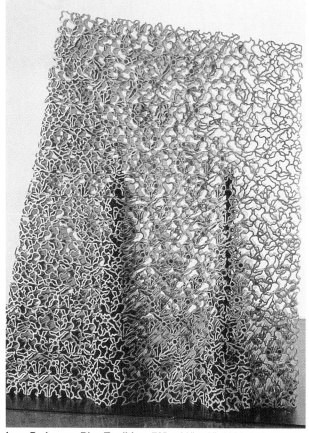

Inge Pedersen, Blue Tradition, 72" x 68" x 8", 1998, 300 extruded modules, each 5 to 12", connected postfire, stoneware, fired to cone 10. Photo by Terje Agnalt.

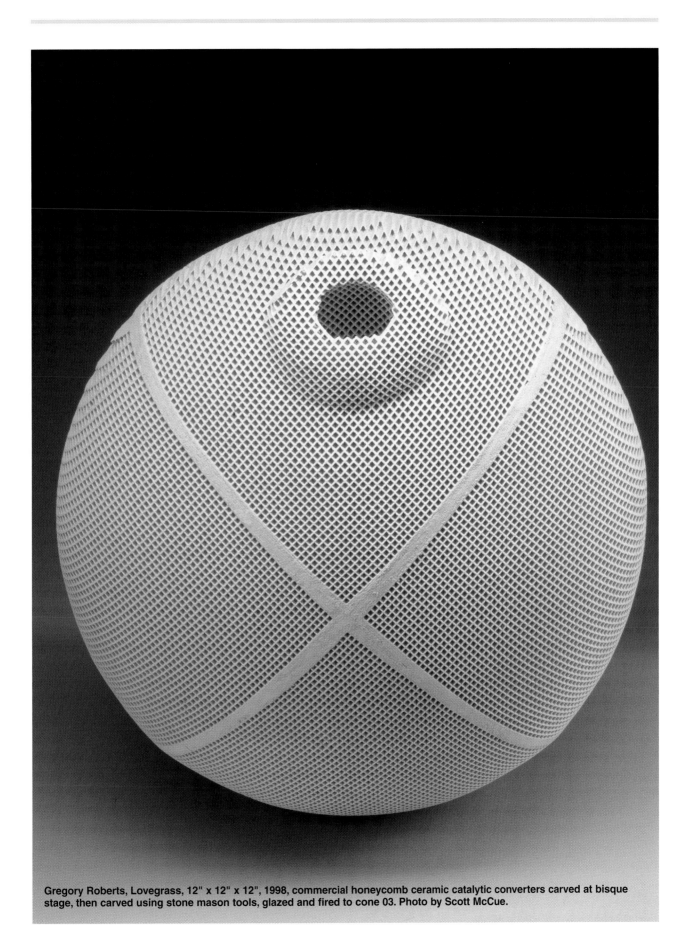

Gregory Roberts, Lovegrass, 12" x 12" x 12", 1998, commercial honeycomb ceramic catalytic converters carved at bisque stage, then carved using stone mason tools, glazed and fired to cone 03. Photo by Scott McCue.

Tom Latka, Can't Stand Still, 36" x 18" x 18", 1989, extruded bottom, thrown top, glued together after cone 01 oxidation firing.

Gladys Soued, Suspension, 12" x 10", 1999, curved bowl die extrusion attached to base, raku fired to cone 010. Photo by John Lackenby.

Tom Latka, Octipot, 14" x 10" x 9", 1978, bottom extruded from an X die and altered, fired with majolica glaze to cone 01, top thrown, coated with latex, and sandblasted, pieces glued together after firing.

Gene H. Koss, Model, 24" x 24" x 9", 1977, extruded coils, fired to cone 10 reduction. Photo by the artist.

Brenda Richardson, Caged Ball, 14" x 14" x 14", 1993, square extruded shapes assembled and painted with low-fire stains and glazes, fired to cone 03. Photo by Deborah Powers.

Natalie Surving, Untitled, 14" x 10" x 9", 1999, fired to cone 03 oxidation. "I began experimenting in using extruded hollow forms as a basis for sculpture and use them extensively." Photo by the artist.

Mary D. Guidetti, Sea Whelk, 32" x 22" x 21", 1993, large altered extruded tube, fired to cone 03 oxidation. Photo by the artist.

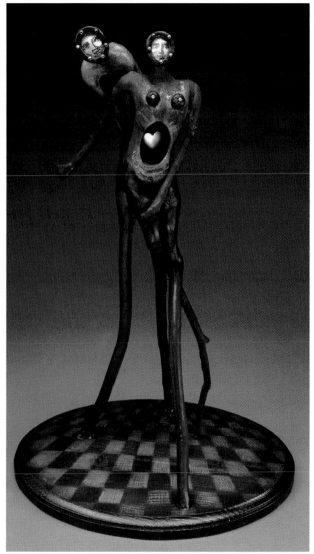

Marie Gibbons, The Couple, 28" x 10" x 6", extruded tube altered to form hollow torsos, legs added postfiring by attaching tree branches, faces of ink on paper glued over clay, fired to cone 010 raku. Photo by John Bonath.

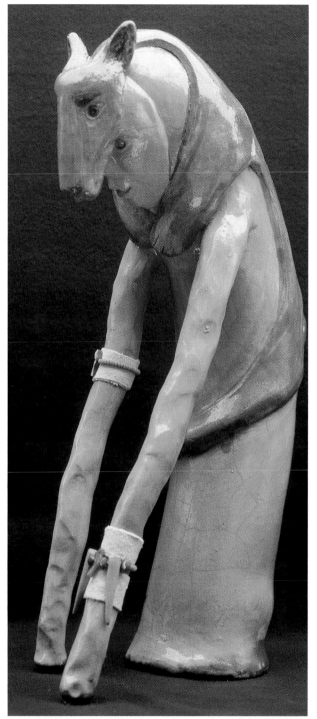

Genie Thomsen, Coyote Dancer, 13" x 5" x 5", 1989, fired to cone 03 oxidation. Photo by the artist.

Tom Latka, Shards, 6' x 5' x 8", 1988, extruded slabs and hand-built coils, fired to cone 03 oxidation, postfire decoration with acrylics.

Edith Murphy, Pod Grouping, 32" x 32" x 34", 1995, extrusions combined with thrown forms, low-fire salt bisque. Photo by the artist.

Rimas T. Visgirda, To Tea or Not to Tea, 16" x 16" x 6", earthenware, fired to cone 03 oxidation. Photo by the artist.

Rina Peleg, Artpark, 5' x 6' x 4', 1982, extruded coils woven to create life-size sculpture, fired to cone 03 oxidation. Photo by the artist.

Jerry Caplan, Torso, 5' x 2' x 2', 1994, industrial extrusion, soaked with wet cloth and altered, fired to cone 10 reduction. Photo by the artist.

Joe Triplo, Untitled, 3' x 2', 1978, extruded assembly, fired to cone 04. Photo by Dave Palmer.

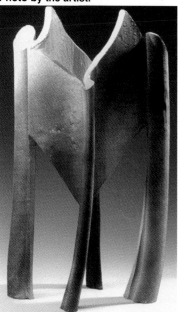

Tom Latka, Precipice, 12" x 6" x 6", 1978, cut extruded form, earthenware, fired to cone 03.

Tom Latka, Persuasion, each 6' x 18" x 4", 2000, extrusions incorporated with commercial tile and slumped at cone 10.

Paris Marie, To Be or Not to Be a Basket, 36" x 18" x 9", 1983, extruded coils altered and combined with asymmetrical thrown form, fired to cone 010 in sagger flash fire. Photo by the artist.

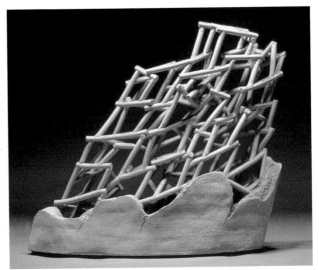

Joanne Hayakawa, Perilous Fortitude, 32" x 10" x 27", 1989, extruded assemblage, stoneware, fired to cone 8. Photo by the artist.

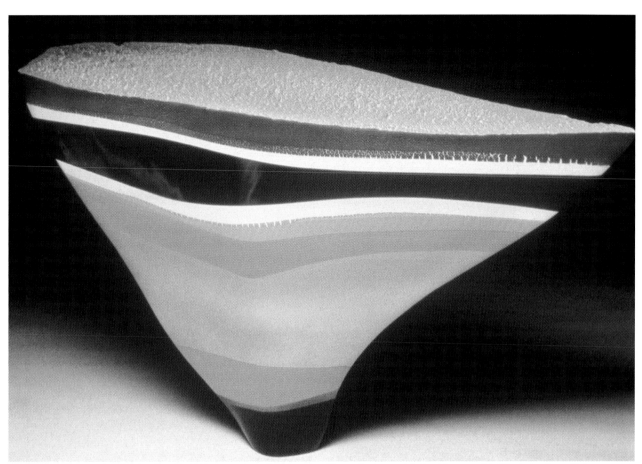

Nick Latka, Tsunami, 24" x 218" x 4", 1991, extruded slabs pressed into plaster mold, fired to cone 01. Photo by the artist.

M. Aktal, Wall Piece, 2' x 2', 1982, extruded slabs made into tiles, fired to cone 01, acrylic decoration added. Photo by the artist.

M. Aktal, Blast to Heaven, 4' x 6' x 2", 1999, extruded forms cut open to make slabs, fired to cone 03 with acrylic paint added after fire. Photo by the artist.

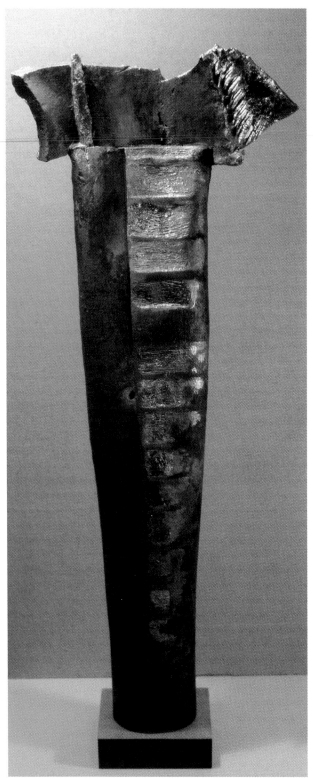

Tom Latka, Teapot, 18" x 10" x 8", 1981, combination of extruded forms combined with wheel-thrown form and assembled after firing to cone 010, sagger flash fire.

Jerry Caplan, Icon, 6' x 2' x 1', 1995, industrial extruded sewer pipe altered into sculptural form, fired to cone 10. Photo by the artist.

Tom Latka, Slipping Away, 12" x 12" x 9", 1999, commercial tile with extrusions added, slumped in fire to cone 10, fused glass and stone.

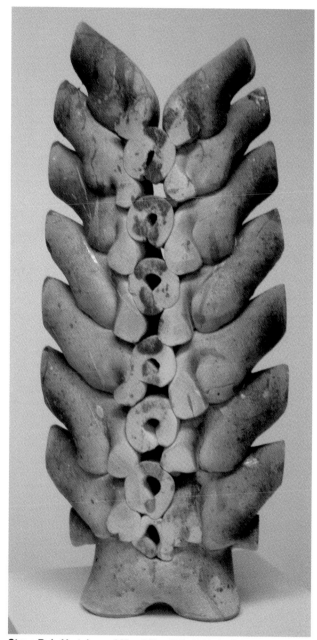

Steve Bair, Vertebrae, 36" x 14" x 14", 1988, individual extruded pieces altered and combined with hand built substructure, fired to cone 010, sagger flash fire. Photo by the artist.

Priscilla Hoback, Sconce Light, 8" x 8" x 24", 1979, six-sided extruded form cut in half, fired to cone 10. Photo by the artist.

George Tomkins, Summit Brick, Pueblo, Colorado, 6' x 8' x 4", 1976, extruded industrial forms manipulated into sculptural form, unfired. Photo by the artist.

Tom Latka, Dancer, 36" x 18" x 18", 1999, hollow extruded form added to top of slab which is lid for a thrown form, fired to cone 01.

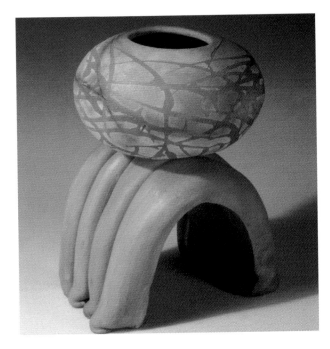

Susanne Stephenson, Untitled, 25½" x 10" x 8", 1983, wheel-thrown form combined with extruded forms on base to create a dramatic foot, porcelain with colored slips, fired to cone 10. Photo by John Stephenson.

Tom Latka, Arched Vessel, 12" x 8" x 8", 1997, series of hollow extrusions joined together with thrown form top, fired to cone 01. Photo by Jean Eskra.

Phillip Sellers, Untitled, 14" x 10" x10", 1997, extruded straps woven in basket, handles stained with clay body and manganese mixture, fired to cone 5, oxidation. Photo by Jerry Anthony.

Problem: The extrusion doesn't come out of the die straight.

♦ This can happen if:
- The die is not lined up exactly in the middle of the barrel. To correct it, align the die so it is centered.
- There's an obstruction in the die such as hardened clay, rocks, or something that doesn't belong. This will cause the clay to circumvent the blockage and exit the machine in another place. Correct this by removing the die and cleaning the extruder, removing the blockage.
- More clay comes out one side of the die hole than the other. To correct this, make certain the die is aligned in the center of the barrel.
- The beginning of the extrusion curls as it exits the machine. Sometimes if you just keep going, the weight of the extrusion will straighten it out (gravity in action).

Problem: Dog Ear - the clay tears along the edges as it exits the die.

♦ This can happen if:
- There are sharp (acute) angles on the die. Increase the angle in the die and experiment until it is possible to extrude without the dog ear. This is a case where it is necessary to modify the die and find the optimum angle where dog ears are eliminated and you achieve the angle you want.
- There is too much friction between the clay and the die. This is usually caused by clay that is too dry or too coarse. Use a wetter clay that has less grog.
- Soft clay is introduced on top of hard clay or vice versa. To correct this, first pug the clay you want to extrude with. This will provide you with a well homogenized clay.
- The clay exits faster on one side of the die than another. Make certain the die hole is centered in the middle of the die and that the die is centered in the middle of the barrel.
- The clay is too short and tears. Use clay that is well homogenized, soft, and with less grog.
- The die needs a beveled edge. Bevel the interior edges of all the dies to a 45° angle.

Problem: The extrusion falls off the machine too early.

♦ This can happen if:
- The clay is too short or coarse. Switch to a clay that is softer and has less grog.
- The clay is too wet. Use a clay that has had time to stiffen and become harder.

A vertical pottery pugmill extruder from the studio of Eric Norstad, circa 1920s. Photo by David Porter.

- There's a disparity between wet and dry clay. Create a consistent clay by either pugging it or wedging it before use.
- There's air trapped in the extrusion. This occurs predominantly in a plunger-type extruder, so it is necessary to pack the clay tightly in the barrel before beginning to extrude.
- The extrusion is too heavy or too long. Either switch to a stiffer clay or make the extrusions the length possible with the clay you are using.

Problem: The extruder is difficult to clean.

♦ When clay sticks to the barrel, you will have a hard time cleaning it. In plunger-type extruders, spray the inside of the barrel and expansion box with a light coating of WD 40 oil before packing clay in the extruder. This coating between the clay and the metal barrel enables the clay to simply peel away from the sides of the barrel.

Problem: Clay has dried inside the pugmill barrel.

♦ The best way to solve this problem is to prevent it from happening. If the clay has dried, pour a cup of water into the hopper mouth and let it sit overnight. Repeat the process until the clay has softened and you can remove it.

Nils Lou at his self-designed "Pneumo Struder," a vertical pneumatic power plunger extruder. Photo courtesy of the artist.

John Glick at his custom-made horizontal plunger extruder. Photo by the artist.

Jack Sures at his hydraulic powered vertical plunger extruder. Photo by Frank Leroy.

David Hendley's homemade manual plunger extruder. Photo by the artist.

◆ On a vertical pugmill when the clay has become too hard, remove the dies, turn the machine on, and let it run. The dried clay will exit the machine in chunks. Then remove the barrel for further cleaning.

Problem: Small extrusions from a plunger-type extruder are difficult to extrude.
◆ This will happen if:
  - The clay is too hard. Use softer, more plastic clay.
  - There's not enough leverage available to power the clay from the die. In this case, get a longer lever which might necessitate stronger dies.

Problem: The extrusion distorts as it is removed from the machine.
◆ If this happens, chances are your clay is too soft. Use harder clay.

Problem: The extrusion is unworkable, breaking and cracking after it is off the machine.

◆ It's likely the clay is too short, coarse, or dry. Use a more plastic, softer clay.

Problem: Cracks develop during the drying or firing stage.
◆ This can happen if:
  - Drying is uneven. Dry the work more slowly and evenly.
  - The clay pieces are not adequately joined together. To prevent this, score and slip all junctions and dry them slowly.

Problem: The dies break in the machine.
◆ Clay that is too hard will break dies. Change to a softer, more plastic clay or use a larger, stronger die.

Problem: Clay oozes out the edges between the barrel and the die mounting system.
◆ This will happen if the die mounting system is not adequately attached to the barrel. If possible, tighten the die

Colin Kellam's hydraulic powered vertical plunger extruder.
Photo by the artist.

Michael Sherrill throwing from his custom-designed electric
vertical plunger extruder. This extruder sits on bearings and
can be spun free or locked in place. The foot that compresses
the clay is a screw jack. Sherrill turns the extruder to the down
position and the acme thread revolves and pushes clay
through the extruder and die. When he wants the clay to
revolve, he unlocks the barrel, which allows him to control the
extruder like a normal potter's wheel. Photo by Margery
Sherrill.

mounting system. If not, use additional C-clamps.

Problem: Hollow extrusions split as they exit the machine.

♦ A common cause of splitting extrusions is an interior die bridge that's too close to the exit hole. The clay does not have time to rejoin and mesh with itself before leaving the extruder. To correct this, redesign the die and position the bridge further away from the exit hole.

Problem: It's difficult to manually force the clay out of the plunger extruder with an expansion box.

♦ This can happen if:
- There's not enough power for the larger extrusion out. Expansion boxes are really for power extruders. If you're having this problem, you'll probably have to remove the expansion box and

use the small manual extruder as it was meant to be used.
- The clay is too hard. In this case, switch to a more plastic clay.

Problem: You want to use your computer to design more complex dies.

♦ Artist Bob Pike uses a Mac G3 300 Mghz computer to design molds for jiggering and extruding. He explains, "I first draw a design for the die on paper and scan it into Adobe Illustrator. After the template is complete, I run it through a translation program called Bezarc (by Kandu software, approximately $400). This program translates Illustrator files into DXF or DDES2 files that are needed for laser cutting." Take the files to a machinist who has a laser cutter and a program that can read your files. They can then cut the dies from 3/16" steel.

Jim Robison at his studio. Robison chose to make it wider than the traditional vertical plunger extruder.

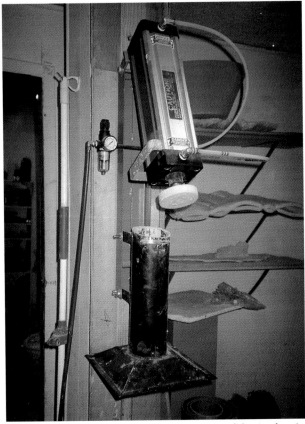

Macy Dorf has combined parts of two commercial extruders to form one hybrid that meets his needs. Photo courtesy of the artist.

This type of hand operated extruder uses gears to push the clay through the extruder. All the components are the same as the manual lever extruder except the lever is replaced with a circular handle. When this handle is turned, the gears force the plunger down, which pushes the clay down the barrel and out.

Ceramic Extruding

Chapter 8
Studio Safety

Your studio can be the one creative outlet in your life. It can also be the most lethal. Unless precautions are taken to ensure a safe, hazard-free environment, chances are you could come down with a litany of problems that, at the least, could force you to change your occupation or hobby. Put simply, it pays to be alert and to clean up after yourself.

The most obvious danger in a studio is free particle dust floating in the air. You may think it's enough to leave the studio after a cleaning and wait until the dust settles before resuming work. The problem is that microscopic particles remain airborne for a minimum of 24 hours before they completely settle. And, as soon as someone walks through the room, lifts a sheet of plastic, or opens a fresh bag of clay, these particles can be back in the air.

Is it impractical to create a studio that is dust free? Probably, but there are certain steps you can take to minimize particle matter in the air and if these are maintained, you can create a relatively clean environment in your studio.

Water is the secret and using it liberally is the key strategy.

♦ When pottery racks are empty, wipe them down with a damp sponge.
♦ Clean up glaze and clay spills immediately.
♦ Frequently wipe down tables with a damp sponge.
♦ Wash the floor. We do this by pouring a pitcher of water on the floor and mopping it up with a large, restaurant size sponge. Wring the sponge out in a clay bucket, not back into your clean water source.
♦ Wipe down the ware boards, especially after glazing, so that the glaze powder doesn't become airborne.
♦ Seal your ware boards with polyurethane. This will create a nonporous surface that can be easily wiped down with water.
♦ Wash your hands on a regular basis.
♦ Keep clay scraps picked up. Once they dry and get walked on, they turn to a powder which then becomes easily airborne. To remove dry clay from the floor of our studio we use a central vacuum system.

Nan Roche, Open Loop in Loop Necklace, 36" long, polymer clay necklace extruded using caulking gun, fired to 400°. Photo by the artist.

♦ Research and invest in a vacuum. They are more complex than you may think. Many people like to work and vacuum while they are in the studio, which seems reasonable. Spill a bag of grog, vacuum it up. Right? Well, not really. The problem is that the clay particles are so fine that unless they are trapped in a special filter they will simply re-enter the studio through the exhaust flow of the vacuum. OSHA rated HEPPA filters are required on all vacuums that are intended to suck up clay dust. But what happens is that the filter, being so fine, soon clogs up and diminishes the suction power of the vacuum. It's critical to change filters often to maximize both the effectiveness of the vacuum and the quality of the air you and others are breathing. The filters are expensive and when added to the cost of the vacuum, cleaning suddenly becomes a costly undertaking.

We purchased and installed a Beam vacuum system in our studio. The motor, filter, and debris catcher are located outside the back door. Running along the ceiling on the inside of the building is a channel of 1¼" white PVC pipe which connects to the vacuum hose. This, in turn, connects to the vacuum system outside. Plugging in the hose automatically turns on the vacuum. The beauty of this system is that the filter, because of its outdoor location, does not have to meet the stringent requirements for an interior vacuum.

Elina Brandt-Hansen, Spiral, 18" x 18" x 1", 1994, colored porcelain clay extruded through small round die, strips then layered upon each other with black slip between each row, porcelain cone 10 oxidation. Photo by the artist.

John Glick, Pot Holder Wall Sculpture, 18" x 10" x 5", thrown and extruded components, fired to cone 10 reduction. Photo by the artist.

Right: Tom Latka, Oil Can Series, 18" x 12" x 6", 1993, different extrusions manipulated and joined together to make a sculptural statement, fired to cone 01.

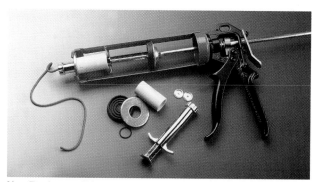

Nan Roche, caulking gun used to power the clay gun to produce the extrusions. In front are shown the adapter parts used along with a clay gun. Photo by the artist.

Rather than trapping the microscopic clay particles, with the Beam system they are free to exit into the atmosphere in the form of fugitive dust, which is a particle size recognized by the Environmental Protection Agency as a component of our planet. We only use the system to vacuum up the clay dust, preferring to wipe up glaze and chemical spills with a sponge so they are not emitted into the air.

When mixing or spraying glazes or clay it is important to wear an OSHA certified respirator with replaceable cartridges that screw onto the mask. Purchase these from a store that specializes in selling certified safety clothing and equipment rather than a general hardware store. These stores can be located in the Yellow Pages of your phone book in the safety section. At the store they will fit and adjust the mask to your face. They also look up the specific dust particles

Judy Moonelis, Untitled, 14" x 18" x 5", 1977, sculpture using hand-building techniques combined with extrusions, earthenware, fired to cone 03. Photo by the artist.

Tom Latka, My Grecian Urn Plus, 22' x 12" x 12", 1999, wheel-thrown base combined with altered extrusion, salt bisque, fired to cone 010.

that you are subjected to and sell you the cartridge for that dust. Most potters think that silica dust is the most toxic but talc is equally as dangerous and can be filtered out through the respirator. Change the cartridges at least as often as is recommended by the manufacturer.

The clay artist's greatest ally and equally great nemesis is fire. Make certain that electric kilns are installed according to the electrical specifications recommended by the manufacturer and by your local building department. Potentially harmful vapors and gases are emitted when firing clay products. Kilns must be well ventilated so the kiln gases are exhausted to the atmosphere. Housing them in an outdoor area, away from the working studio space, is the solution.

If you are building a gas kiln outdoors, locate it away from anything combustible and if you plan to cover it with a roof, construct the roof out of metal. Gas pipes should be checked periodically for leaking. This is done by spraying the joints with a solution of water and dish soap. If there is a leak, it will form air bubbles and should be repaired immediately. Position the main gas valve away from the kiln and easily accessible in case you need to shut it down in an emergency. When you are firing the kiln with propane, which is a heavy gas, the tank should be a minimum of 20' from the kiln and in an open area.

Keep a fire extinguisher in the area where you house

Roy Hanscom, Extruded Box, 8" x 15" x 6", 1998, extrusions cut and shaped to form box, fired to cone 6. Photo by the artist.

Rachel Tzanmir, Untitled, 25" x 40" x 9", 1987, hollow formed extrusion combined with round extrusion, raku, fired to cone 010. Photo by the artist.

Robert Flynn, Box, 10" x 6" x 6", 1993, extrusions modified and assembled to make box forms, stoneware with ash glaze, fired to cone 10. Photo by the artist.

your kilns. Do all raku style firing outdoors as there is volumes of smoke and vapors emitted from the metals. If you have long hair, tie it up and don't wear synthetic clothing.

We routinely melt wax resist in an electric frying pan. Paraffin is flammable and should be melted slowly to ensure that it won't catch on fire.

If you are using asbestos gloves, immediately throw them away, as one airborne particle per million can cause cancer. The asbestos particle is star-shaped and at each pointed end there is a little sharp hook that catches on the lining of the lungs and becomes embedded. Over time the particles irritate the tissue and turn into sores. Use gloves made from cotton or Kevlar 29, a non-asbestos material from DuPont that is flame and heat resistant. Most burns come from overzealous

potters pulling pots from the kiln while they are still very hot.

Be kind to your back, since back pain seems to be the primary complaint of clay artists. And it's understandable. Clay people move great quantities of weight. If you mix your own clay, the components come in 50 to 100 pound bags. Even premixed clay comes in 50 pound boxes. Then there are the ware boards full of pottery, kiln shelves, and boxes or crates of the finished product. It is important to lift with your legs. Squat down, keeping your back straight, and let your legs do the lifting. Avoid twisting your torso while you lift. The abdominal muscles keep the back aligned so doing sit-ups is a good way to keep them toned and in turn, strengthen your back.

Protect your eyes. When looking in the kiln while it is

firing at high temperatures, wear infrared glasses to prevent retina problems. Safety glasses are a must when using machines like grinders, saws, and drills.

Wear rubber gloves while mixing glazes, slips, and stains.

Remember that all machines have the potential to hurt you. Clay machines to be cautious of are the clay mixer (where you can lose an arm), the auger in a pugmill (there goes a finger), the slab roller (smashed fingers), extruders with sharp edges (a few stitches), potter's wheels that have a flywheel (ready to catch your feet and send you flying), and kilns that can burn you.

Keep track of your tools, especially the metal ribs. They are so thin and sharp they become treacherous when mixed inadvertently into a batch of clay, slicing your hand as you dig the clay from the mixer.

Every studio will generate a certain amount of waste, some toxic and some benign. In an effort to maintain an ecological consciousness we have developed methods for dealing with our ceramic wastes. All clay scraps and trimmings are recycled and remixed into workable clay. The pugmill is an excellent tool for reclaiming clay. If this isn't possible, slake the clay down with water and spread it out on canvas sheets to dry. When the clay has dried to a pliable, workable stage, simply roll it up and bag it until ready to use.

Extra glazes that accumulate around the studio are combined, tested, and if it is a mediocre glaze, used on the inside of vessels and pots. Edith Heath's pottery in Sausolito, Calif., mixes their extra glazes in the clay to flux the body.

A great hazard to plumbing systems is sending glaze, oxides, or clay down the sewers. To avoid this, rinse your brushes in a glass jar. Stains and oxides will accumulate at the bottom of the jar and when mixed together make a beautiful black oxide which is perfect for brush work. We weighed what we had recycled over a four month period and it was about five pounds, which is a substantial amount. To clean buckets and other tools, use a designated water barrel that is at least 30 gallons. Do a preliminary wash in the barrel, removing the majority of the glaze or clay. Then a final wash can be done in the sink. About every four months we clean out the barrel by siphoning off the clean water on top. The waste that has accumulated at the bottom of the barrel is poured into bisque vessels that are 12" high with walls at least 3/8" thick and fired to cone 10 where they are rendered stable, inert, and harmless.

Carpal tunnel syndrome, the numbing of the fingers, seems to be a current affliction. Michael Cardew, who was a potter in the 1930s, said he and his peers never experienced carpal tunnel because they always made their own clay and its consistency was generally a soft clay. He attributed the problem to commercial, premixed clay that is often too hard to throw. The solution is to mix your own clay or, if this is not possible, tell your clay supplier to mix you a wetter, softer clay. If you purchase small quantities, repug the clay and add water during the process.

Most materials are harmful when ingested. This applies equally to many common household materials as well as those of the pottery and art departments. Don't eat or drink in the studio. Calcium and lithium are not the same compounds you find in the health food store. Wash your hands before you bite your nails.

The danger of lead poisoning is still a major concern in this country. Avoid even bringing lead into your studio because chances are, no matter how careful you are, it will get out and contaminate something. Lead oxide, lead carbonate, and galena (lead sulfide) are all soluble and poisonous. Many Mexican potters use lead as a flux in their glazed ware and it is important to avoid using these pots for food or drink.

All materials need be handled with care but there are some that deserve special mention - barium carbonate, enamels, borax, boric acid, silica, zinc oxide, lusters, ceramic glazes generally but particularly those containing cadmium, selenium, lithium, antimony oxide, and copper and nickel compounds. Other materials that are toxic and need to be handled with caution are all the cadmium compounds, chrome and chromate compounds, manganese dioxide, nickel compounds, and vanadium pentoxide. Chemicals that irritate the lungs include all the copper compounds, cobalt colorants, zinc oxide, zirconium compounds, bone ash, calcium, sodium borate, silica, talc (calcium, magnesium silicate), and wollastonite (calcium silicate).

Now that you are aware of some of the concerns that wait for you in your studio, remember that they are harmless if you address them properly. It's not knowing that is truly harmful. Go create, have fun, and be safe.

Chapter 9
The Business of Art

Tom Latka, Steppin' Out, 18" x 5" x 5", 1997, extruded base combined with wheel-thrown top, fired to cone 01.

T wenty years ago we had a fantasy of becoming self-employed artists, making our livelihood selling the work we created. Like two glaze-eyed ducks, we waddled into a stream completely unaware of where we were going, how to navigate through the currents and eddies, and not even envisioning where we might end up. All we were armed with was a sincere yet naive belief that we were somehow touched by a creative calling that would guide us through the uncharted waters. In retrospect, all we can say is that it was fortunate we had unfathomable energy and a tenacious nature for those two elements carried us through many an undertow where drowning seemed imminent.

We are frequently asked to talk to college students about the business of art, specifically how to become self-employed, full-time working artists or, as we like to say, how to turn clay into bread. The first bit of advice we offer to students is to get used to the word "no." It's only two letters and one syllable but unless you understand how to cope with it, that word can throw your life into the mud.

Many individuals feel a calling to express themselves creatively and to support themselves and their families through their work. We live in an interesting culture that cherishes and acknowledges the importance of the artistic spirit yet political priorities, policies, and attitudes are such that capital improvements rarely include art projects. With an abundance of art professors, a government overspent and underserved, and a public inundated with imports, the artist who wishes to make a living through their work faces interesting challenges.

Not every artist wants to take on the responsibilities and demands of turning their work into a consumer business. Many fear that selling their art compromises the work or that the daily grind of self-promotion diminishes their creative qualities. These are valid considerations and need to be resolved before venturing onward.

A large population of artists do support themselves through their work and in doing so each has developed a method and carved out a niche to promote and sell their

Nancy Hall, Cockeyed Chook Horn, 22" x 24" x 3",1994, earthenware cone 03. "It seems to me that the extruded formed coils are easier to handle and break less than when using hand rolled ones." Photo by the artist.

work. The approaches are as varied as the colors in a sunset. In the last 25 years we have experimented with myriad ways of keeping ourselves self-employed, working as full-time artists and craftspeople.

We have often assumed that what works for someone else will work for us. Big myth. Each person, through intuition and direct learning, discovers the means to enable them to continue their work. Creating the business dimension can become an extension of the art. Naturally, it took us quite a while and thousands of miles in the car to finally understand this.

Retail Sales vs. Wholesale

Wholesale goods are purchased from the artist in quantity and at a reduced price, generally 50%. Most vendors, shops, and galleries buy wholesale and double the price when they sell retail. From the onset of our business, retail sales always made more sense to us. We not only liked getting full market value for the work, but the idea of having to make half as many pots to achieve the same financial goal was very appealing. To avoid the wholesale market, we have tried endless schemes for selling our work at retail and over the years have found a variety of avenues that have proven successful for us.

Hospital Sales

Hospitals are great places for sales because you have

access to hundreds of people under one roof. Contact the hospital's Volunteer Coordinator and propose a pottery sale in the lobby, offering to give 20% of sales to the hospital. Schedule the sale to coincide on or near payday. Send flyers announcing the sale two weeks before the event, instructing the volunteers to stuff them in all employee mailboxes. Also, have them distribute flyers to the patients.

Hospitals love this fundraising idea because it is little work for them and they generate funds. They usually want to make it an annual event. Save names from checks to start a mailing list for next year's sale. We do a series of these in the fall and through the Christmas season and can always expect between $3,000 to $5,000 per sale.

Annual Studio Sale

We started an Annual Christmas Sale and a Spring Pottery Sale and found them to be the best way to invest in our business and promote our pottery in the community.

Buy a small ad in the local paper. Our ads feature a photo of us, one of our children, or friends. We notice that no matter how small or obscure the location of the ad, people like to look at people and their eyes will be drawn to a photo. Ask the paper to run a story about the event. Take advantage of any free listings offered by community calendars. Contact the radio and television stations and invite them to the opening.

After the sale, start a mailing list using checks or a sign-in book and keep it current. Mailed announcements are

Virginia McClure, detail, 1987, extruded coils used to make large vessel, fired to earthenware cone 03. Photo by the artist.

expensive and only about 15% of the people who get them will come, but they do keep your name in their minds for other purchases.

Summer Craft Shows and Fairs

Like many artists starting out, we did summer fairs and found them both depressing and exhausting because we never did very well at them. It always seemed that someone three booths down had more commercially appealing pots and better prices and their booth would be wall to wall people. However, these shows did manage to keep us in enough cash flow so we could return to the studio and make more pots. (One reason we are still potters is that we kept making pots and kept getting better at it.)

Avoid events where the art/craft market is not the primary focus. We were once invited to set up a booth and sell at the "Always Buy Colorado" fair in the Denver Coliseum. The estimated attendance was in the neighborhood of 100,000 for the weekend and we thought we might need to drive two vehicles: one to bring home the display and one to bring home all the money we would make. That's how convinced we were that we were going to finally witness mass hysteria at our pottery booth. We sold one mug.

It is our experience that we do not sell our work in situations where people stumble upon art between the cheese giveaway and the free long distance phone calls. Hence, we only do shows that are advertised as artistic events and the people coming to the event know that.

American Craft Exposition and Rosen Shows

Located in strategic cities around the country, these shows are designed to connect artists to wholesale buyers and the buying public. They are expensive to get into (about $40 per application) and rejections run high due to the high number of creative, competent artists who apply. They are also expensive to do. Booth fees vary between $1,000 to $2,000, depending on the location. You must also factor in travel expenses, lodging, food, booth design, and set up costs (it's nice to have a rug in the booth and some artistic backdrops), and printed material like cards and catalogs to hand out or send out to interested buyers.

Should you decide to do a wholesale show, present work that is of a similar theme and concept. These shows are geared for the upscale gift and craft shop. Buyers dash up and down the isles, stopping only if they see items that tickle their fancy. If the booth is too busy and confusing, filled with too many examples and styles for them to readily discern, they simply swoosh past. We have always managed to break even on these shows and attribute our lack of success

Wes Thomas, Oh What a Big Vase You Art, 12" x 6" x 9", 1976, extruded handles pulled to desired form, bottom hand thrown, fired to cone 10 wood fire. Photo by the artist.

Tom and Jean Latka, The Floodwall in progress, Michael Rubal in photo, 2000, extruded slabs rolled on burlap-covered easel.

to the fact that we tried to cram too many different styles into our booth.

Many artists are successful with wholesale shows and you have to prepare yourself for that result too: be ready to fill the orders you take. Most buyers pay 50% up front and the final 50% on delivery. Shops and galleries pay shipping. There are always horror stories about artists hooking up with a big chain department store that orders thousands of pieces, will only pay in full 180 days after the work has been delivered, and the artist goes out of business while waiting for the big pay off. Personally, I have never met any artists who have had this experience, but it's wise to realize that it could happen.

The other artists and crafters you meet at a wholesale show can become wonderful references and friends. There is definitely a bond between the participants that can make the show meaningful and memorable.

Trading

Many artists consider trading art for other services to be a real plus in the budgeting of life's amenities. Most professionals enjoy trading because they feel they are getting more in exchange than their dollar would buy. Plus, they end up with things that they might not have otherwise purchased. I have heard of trades that almost reach the surreal:

prenatal care, library fines, tuxedo rentals, doctor care, birthday parties, supplies, pet food, hotels, drywall hanging and texturing.

Sometimes proposing a trade can be awkward because people feel like they are put on the spot and trapped by the request. To avoid this, if we know we need a particular service we send letters to people who provide that service, telling of our need and desire to trade. We enclose photos of our work and explain how the trade is accomplished. Then we wait for someone to call. If we don't hear from anyone by the end of the week we do a follow up call.

Donating Your Art

Every nonprofit organization will approach you to donate work for their endeavors. We always give something, generally a bowl, because it is a good way to get work into the community and seen by a variety of people. Before saying yes, ask if the organization would be willing to split the profits from the sale of the piece. This is becoming more popular in certain fundraising groups.

Galleries

If they love you, meaning if your work sells, there can be no better place for your work. Galleries will promote you, stage you, wine and dine you, write articles about your

Tom and Jean Latka, The Floodwall, 2000, extruded slabs and coils used to hand build three-dimensional mural, fired to cone 10 in reduction.

work, plaster you in ads. But if your work doesn't sell after 90 days, you may find your pieces in the back room, under a table. Hopefully the gallery personnel will remember your name when you come to pick up the work. Chances are, though, they won't telephone you with the dismal news, so you'll need to stay on top of the situation. We have had galleries close up without a notice, taking our work with them and leaving no forwarding address.

Established galleries like to discover their stable of artists themselves but are willing to look at new work on the fourth full moon when the sun is in Jupiter and the Pleides are just passing the cusp of Aquarius.

Art Cooperatives

Art cooperatives are organizations run and operated by a group of artists in the interest of selling their work at a commission less than what a typical gallery owner might charge. This can be an excellent selling situation and symbiotic for both the shop and the artists. Coops are structured in a democratic manner, usually requiring annual dues plus shifts where everyone works the store and they take an average commission fee of 30%.

Books

There are a variety of reference books that are distributed to architects and designers for use in working with clients who are in the process of building or remodeling interior and exterior spaces. Artists can purchase a page or pages in the book. In addition to being in the book, the artist

will receive anywhere from 1,000 to 2,000 reproductions of their page. These are handy promotions. Beautifully published on fine, slick paper with exceptional color reproductions, these books are costly to buy into. They do motivate an artist to get fantastic photographs of their work and to write text about themselves. Of all the artists who have invested in this promotional method, our research has shown that only a small percentage actually receive significant commissions and contacts from the publications.

In closing, we want to reiterate that talent is a gift, regardless if it's used to generate income or as a weekend respite to revitalize and refuel one's creative energies. To keep the art alive, the river flowing between the heart, head, and hands, and to believe in the process of creating is the challenge. In every creative act, every song sung in the shower, every poem muttered while falling asleep, there resides a truth and hope for tomorrow.

Public Art Commissions

The last few years have seen a new boom in our security level as we learn about yet another artistic dimension - public art. Colorado is fortunate to have an aggressive public art policy that designates 1% of a state building's construction budget to incorporate art in the building. This includes everything from a heat pumping station at the prison to a new addition at a university, and every Colorado artist is eligible.

Getting into the public art arena can be a tricky situation

Tom and Jean Latka, detail of The Floodwall. Photo by Margo Marie.

since you must have examples of work to photograph to be a contender in the initial selection process. All Colorado artists who are registered with the Colorado Council on the Arts and Humanities receive information about the proposed construction of all public buildings and can apply by sending in slides of their work for consideration. Usually the art selection committee will narrow the group of applicants down to three artists, provide them each with a small stipend, and request a conceptual design for the area. On a predetermined date you take your concepts to the panel and explain them. If they like the ideas, you get to build the piece. If not, better luck next time.

This opportunity to design and present a concept for consideration can prove to be essential in learning how to put together a strong, influential presentation. Many artists use computer presentations complete with digital photos of the art piece superimposed into the area. I have heard of one occasion where the artist supplied background music to augment the presentation.

Many states and cities utilize a similar selection process as the one in Colorado. Some of these encourage both out-of-state and local artists to apply for public art commissions. It is important to register with these different art organizations to ensure that you receive information about their projects. The majority of them have web pages where you can gain information about their guidelines.

About the Authors

Tom and Jean Latka have been professional studio artists for the last 24 years. They live and work in Pueblo, Colorado, with their three children. Tom is a graduate of the University of California at Fullerton. Jean is a self-taught potter. They have contributed numerous articles on pottery and sculpture to ceramic publications and have won many prizes for their ceramic work, which can be found in private and corporate collections, public spaces, and galleries throughout the U.S. The Latkas present workshops nationally on their unique brand of ceramics, which incorporates functional pottery, sculpture, and murals. More of their work can be seen at **www.ceramicsite.com**.

Asymmetry - that which is not symmetrical.

Barrel - part of the extruder where the clay resides before being pushed through the die and out of the machine.

Auger - helical screw that moves the clay through the chamber and out of the extruder.

Bridge - sturdy pieces of metal that connect hollow dies to the extruder.

Chamber - another name for the barrel of the extruder.

Die - wood, plastic, or metal plate containing the hole or holes through which the clay is forced. The shape of the die determines the shape of the extrusion.

Expansion Box - an extension attached to the end of the barrel to allow for larger extrusions.

Extrusion - clay shaped by the die in an extruder.

Feed Bevel - the area around the lip of the die beveled at a 45° angle so that the clay is angled into the hole of the die.

Grog - fired clay that has been ground and sifted to particle size. It is introduced into clay bodies to reduce shrinkage and add color.

Hopper Mouth - opening where clay is put into the extruder.

Line Symmetry - when only one line can be drawn down the center of any two-dimensional object, creating a mirror image.

Plasticity -

Plunger Extruder - manually operated extruder composed of a chamber with a piston. It is operated by inserting clay into the barrel and forcing the plunger down until the clay is forced out through the die.

Plunger Plate - bottom of the plunger that meets with the clay.

Point Symmetry - when any line can be drawn anywhere through the center of a two- dimensional shape. However, each side is not a mirror but is a direct replica of the other half.

Pug - to mix clay using a pugmill, to machine grind and knead clay with water into a plastic consistent extrusion. Although it doesn't replace wedging entirely, it does about 90% of the job.

Pugmill Extruder - pugmill adapted to also function as an extruder. This machine blends hard and soft clay into a homogenous slug by forcing clay through a screen and down a chamber by way of an auger. It can also take the air out of the clay and in general makes the clay ready for throwing, jiggering, or pressing. If the clay is not too dry, putting it through a pugmill will recondition and consolidate it, allowing clay to be reclaimed. When dies are attached to the exit orifices, different shapes can be extruded. Bricks, sewer pipes, and chimney flues are some industrial products made with pugmill extruders.

Symmetry - the exact correspondence of form and configuration on opposite sides of a dividing line or plane or about a center or axis.

Wad, Sod or Pug Box - method of making quantities of coils.

Wedging - to hand knead clay until it is completely homogenized and de-aired.

Appendix 2
Extrude a Kiln
by Tom Latka

What does one do when they find their left leg locked in a cast, from hip to toe, for six weeks? Such was my scenario. Learning to navigate on crutches was a necessary pursuit but one that quickly bored me. I needed something challenging, invigorating, a quest that could hold my interest and be simultaneously productive. I decided to take my extruder to new realms by designing and building a kiln made from extruded bricks.

The criteria for the kiln would be straightforward: an easy to load, 60-cubic-foot, downdraft, low-fire salt kiln. Since personal challenge was a key ingredient to the project, I wanted to construct a kiln unlike one I had built before. Eventually I settled on a top-loading cylinder, 4' in diameter and 4' high. The advantage of a top-loading kiln is that every corner is accessible.

The 6' square foundation consisted of a 2" x 4" frame, filled with wet sand, tamped, and screened level. On top of the sand, I laid cement cinder blocks on their sides, permitting air to pass under the kiln and through the cavities in the blocks. On top of the block, I placed hard brick to form the floor of the kiln. The floor had three fire channels that extended from the ports to the center of the kiln, so the flames could become their own baffle, stifling the flow of air

The finished kiln.

The extruded brick I used to build the kiln, keyed in two directions.

The inside of the kiln, showing the bricks and inside chimney.

The die I used to make the bricks.

Detail of the wench used to move the lid.

The kiln with the lid open.

to create a radiant type of heat.

I made the framework for the kiln from ⅛" Masonite stretched around two ¾" x 4' diameter circles of plywood and sculpted the burner ports out of soft brick and hand thrown cylinders.

I constructed the interior wall of the kiln from hollow bricks extruded from a vertically mounted pugmill. I made the 2" x 2" x 12" bricks of sagger clay and fired them to cone 10, keying them in two directions, top and bottom, so they would expand and contract in the same place after each firing. I stacked four rows of bricks vertically around the template, placing an 8" soft brick adjacent to the extruded brick in each row, forming a super-insulated kiln. I then chinked clay between the joints, inside and out.

To form the frame to hold everything together, I used chicken wire stretched around the kiln and then plastered it with cement mix.

The lid posed a problem. The 4" thick lid of my original design, cast with refractory material, would be too heavy. I settled on using insulating fiber - not an optimal choice because of the health hazards of working with fiber, but I mixed the fiber with clay to keep the particles from becoming airborne. I cast a mixture of 90% fiber and 10% fire clay over a dome of sand atop the kiln template.

Bob Dixon, Vase, 29" x 10" x 10", 1999, extruded appendages with hand-thrown pot, fired to cone 10 reduction. Photo by the artist.

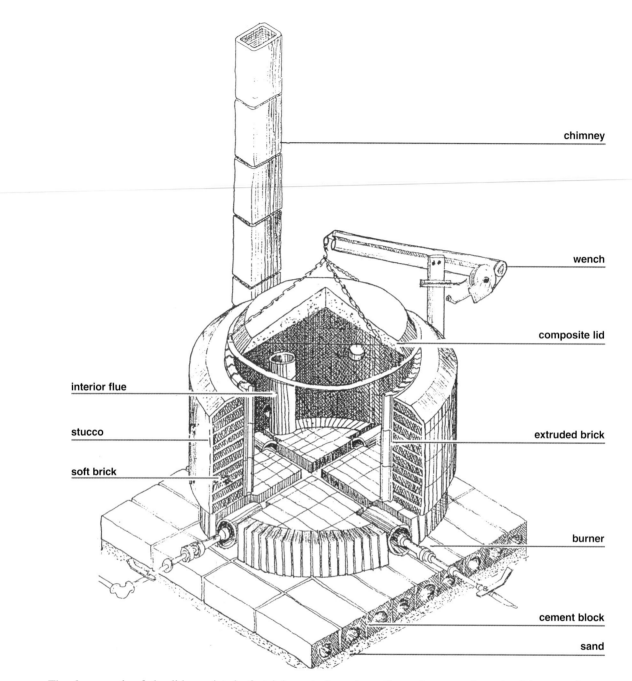

chimney

wench

composite lid

interior flue

stucco

soft brick

extruded brick

burner

cement block

sand

The framework of the lid consisted of stainless steel bicycle spokes radiating from the center outward to a 1" x 1" x 4' diameter steel collar. At three points on the steel collar I welded steel hoops to attach chains that met at the center. The lid moved by being hoisted up with a half-ton wench and pivoted to one side.

I installed Killiam burners for propane fuel. For the stack I used 6" x 8" flue liners held together with baling wire.

My original intent for the kiln was to fire one-of-a-kind salt bisque vessels and wall pieces. Deep in the heart of Mexico, in the state of Oaxaca, potters use flash fire to decorate their pottery. They call this process "Fuego Nube," meaning fire cloud. This term dates back 1,000 years, describing the process scientifically and poetically. The most dramatic results come from the firing pots in saggers with organic material packed around them. Strips of fine copper telephone wire tied around each piece yield a line of black and a hint of green or pink. Any metal that touches the piece produces some color, so I experimented with everything from steel wool to scraps of iron. Organic material such as dirt yields black to gray, similar to raku post-reduction. Egg shells give spots of white and banana peels a light green.

The main supply of carbon comes from straw soaked in salt and dried, providing a rich reddish tan to light tan. After the straw has been packed in the sagger, I sprinkle in a few grains of road salt. I have done nearly 100 firings and all is well.

A. Monque, Square Sculpture, 18" x 16" x 10", 1994, combined extruded shapes, fired to cone 010 raku. Photo by the artist.

Hwang Jeng-daw, Teapot, 10" x 5" x 6", 2000, extruded and rolled teapot spout, colored clay and black glaze, fired to cone 9. Photo by the artist.

John Alliston, Two Aroma Therapy Vaporizers, 7" x 4" x 4", fired to cone 10 with Tenmoku glaze. Photo by Ian Barber.

Appendix 3
Build an Expansion Box
for Pugmill Extruder

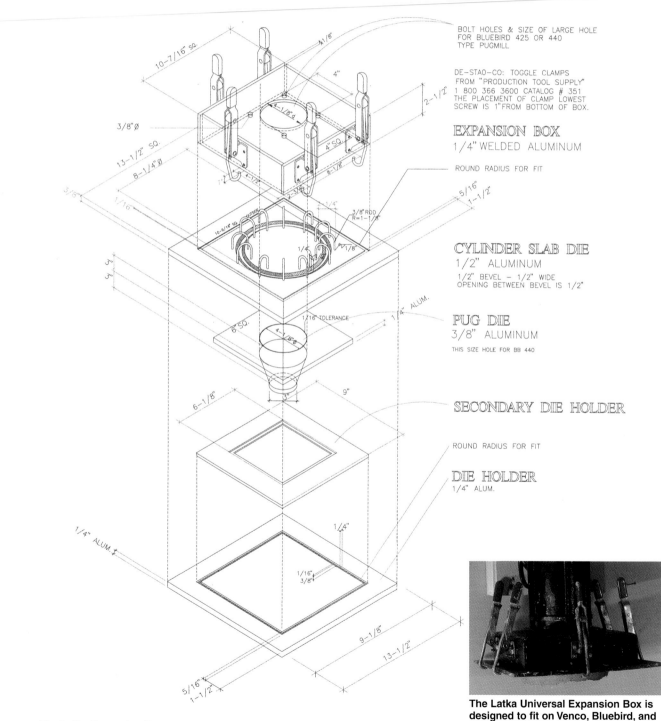

BOLT HOLES & SIZE OF LARGE HOLE
FOR BLUEBIRD 425 OR 440
TYPE PUGMILL

DE-STA0-CO: TOGGLE CLAMPS
FROM "PRODUCTION TOOL SUPPLY"
1 800 366 3600 CATALOG # 351
THE PLACEMENT OF CLAMP LOWEST
SCREW IS 1"FROM BOTTOM OF BOX.

EXPANSION BOX
1/4" WELDED ALUMINUM

ROUND RADIUS FOR FIT

CYLINDER SLAB DIE
1/2" ALUMINUM
1/2" BEVEL – 1/2" WIDE
OPENING BETWEEN BEVEL IS 1/2"

PUG DIE
3/8" ALUMINUM
THIS SIZE HOLE FOR BB 440

SECONDARY DIE HOLDER

ROUND RADIUS FOR FIT

DIE HOLDER
1/4" ALUM.

10-7/16" SQ.
3/8" Ø
13-1/2" SQ.
8-1/4" Ø
3/8"
1/16"
4"
2-1/2"
4" SQ.
8-1/8"
4-1/2"
3/8"
1/8"
5/16"
1-1/2"
1/4"
3/8"ROD
R=1-1/8"
10-3/16"SQ
1/8"
3"
3"
8" SQ.
1/16 TOLERANCE
1/4" ALUM.
4-1/8"Ø
3"
9"
6-1/8"
1/4"
1/16"
3/8"
1/4" ALUM.
9-1/8"
13-1/2"
5/16"
1-1/2"

The Latka Expansion Box.

The Latka Universal Expansion Box is
designed to fit on Venco, Bluebird, and
Shimpo pugmills.

Appendix 4
Sources

Amaco/Brent Extruder
American Art Clay Co., Inc.
4717 W. 16th St.
Indianapolis, IN 46222
phone: 800-374-1600, outside U.S. 317-244-6871
email: catalog@amaco.com
website: AMACO.com

Laguna Clay
14400 Lomitas Ave.
City of Industry, CA 91746
phone: 800-452-4862
email: info@lagunaclay.com
website: www.lagunaclay.com

Mile Hi Ceramics
77 Lipan St.
Denver, CO 80223
phone: 303-825-4570
email: Info@MileHiCeramics.com
website: www.milehiceramics.com

Scott Creek Pottery
2636 Pioneer Way E.
Tacoma, WA 98404
phone: 800-939-8783
fax: 253-922-5349
email: clayextruder@scottcreekpottery.com
website: www.scottcreekpottery.com

Venco Pugmills
29 Owen Road
Kelmscott WA 6111
Australia
phone: 61-8-9-399-5265
fax: 61-8-9-497-1335

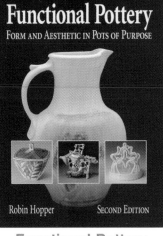
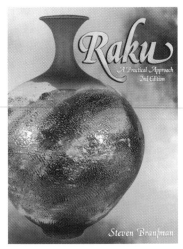

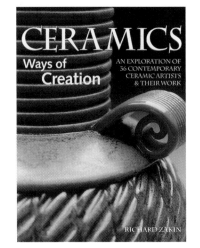
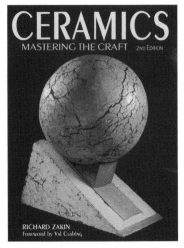